M'LISS RAE HAWLEY

Mariner's
Medallion Quilts

- Creative **No-Math** Approach

- **Blocks & Borders to Mix & Match**

- **Full-Size Compass Foundations**

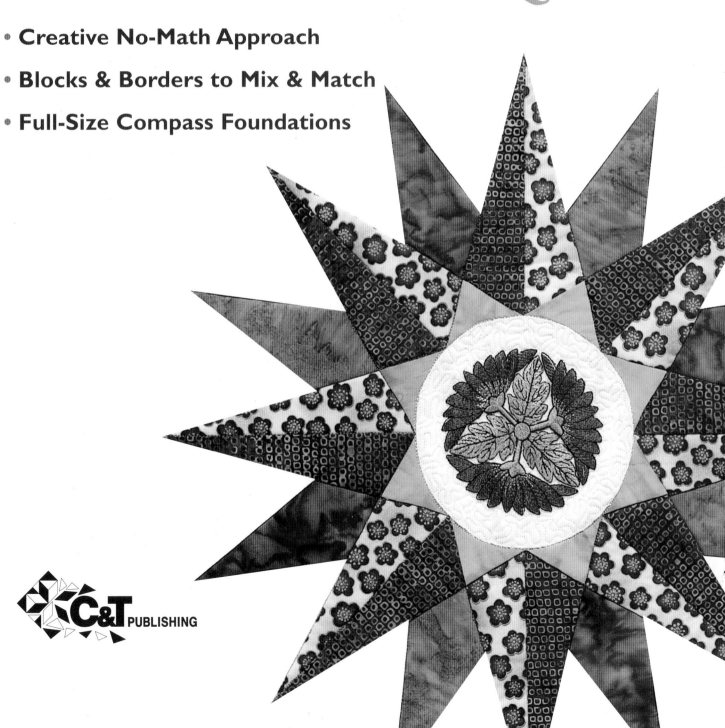

C&T PUBLISHING

Text © 2006 M'Liss Rae Hawley

Artwork © 2006 C&T Publishing, Inc.

Publisher: Amy Marson

Editorial Director: Gailen Runge

Acquisitions Editor: Jan Grigsby

Editor: Darra Williamson

Technical Editors: Helen Frost and Cynthia Keyes Hilton

Copyeditor/Proofreader: Wordfirm, Inc.

Cover Designer: Kristen Yenche

Design Director/Book Designer: Kristen Yenche

Illustrator: Tim Manibusan

Production Assistant: Kerry Graham

Photography: Luke Mulks and Sharon Risedorph; author photo by Michael Stadler

Published by C&T Publishing, Inc., P.O. Box 1456, Lafayette, CA 94549

Front cover: *Dream Guide* by M'Liss Rae Hawley

Back cover: *My Canvas to the World* by M'Liss Rae Hawley and *Koi in Mariner's Garden* by Anastasia Riordan

Library of Congress Cataloging-in-Publication Data

Hawley, M'Liss Rae,
  Mariner's medallion quilts / M'Liss Rae Hawley.
     p. cm.
  ISBN-13: 978-1-57120-380-9 (paper trade : alk. paper)
  ISBN-10: 1-57120-380-X (paper trade : alk. paper)
  1. Patchwork--Patterns. 2. Quilting--Patterns. 3. Compass in art. I. Title.

TT835.H3468 2006
746.46'041--dc22

2006004842

Printed in China
10 9 8 7 6 5 4 3 2 1

DEDICATION

My journey includes many wonderful people—most important, my husband, Michael. His steadfast support has allowed me to follow my passion, and yes, he's still ironing my fabric!

As his career in law enforcement draws to an end, we look ahead to new opportunities.

The Mariner's Compass, pointing in all directions, will be our guide.

ACKNOWLEDGMENTS

I would like to thank—both personally and professionally—the following people and companies who share my vision, enthusiasm, and love of quilting, and to express my gratitude for their contributions to the industry.

C&T Publishing: Amy Marson, Jan Grigsby, Darra Williamson, Kristen Yenche, and Tim Manibusan

Husqvarna Viking: Stan Ingraham, Sue Hausmann, Nancy Jewell, and Theresa Robinson

In The Beginning Fabrics: Sharon Evans Yenter and Jason Yenter

Hoffman Fabrics: Sandy Muckenthaler

Primedia: Tina Battock and Beth Hayes

Quilters Dream Batting: Kathy Thompson

Robison-Anton Textiles: Bruce Anton and Andreea M. Sparhawk

The Electric Quilt Company: Penny McMorris

Tony Kowal, my embroidery specialist: Thank you for your friendship, patience, and creativity.

Contents

Ten years ago, in my first book on the Mariner's Compass motif, I wrote:

I live on an island. It's the right size: not so large that you forget you are surrounded by water, yet not so small that the sea dominates. My island, Whidbey, sits at the entrance to Puget Sound, a short three miles of salt water from the urban congestion of metropolitan Seattle. By day, the view from my studio deck includes skyscrapers, mountains, and whitecaps.

I can also view the many trees we have planted, including lodgepole pines, Douglas firs, and hundreds of filbert trees. Our trees, fields, flowers, and water attract many birds, including one of my favorites, Canada geese.

At night, the rhythmic crisscrossing of lighthouse beams dances across the clouds. In the early-morning stillness, before the fog has lifted, there is no view. None except those painted in my mind by the groans of distant horns warning mariners of dangerous shoals.

Much has changed since I wrote these words; much has remained the same. The trees have grown and so too our children, but while the pines and firs remain, our son and daughter have taken root elsewhere. Alexander spent most of his enlistment overseas, including a year in Iraq leading a Marine Corps rifle platoon. He began in Fallujah and moved on throughout the country—an almost indescribably gut-wrenching time for Michael, our family, and me. He's back now, re-enlisted, and stationed in California. Adrienne has graduated from Seattle University and is making plans for her future. Michael and I have many plans too, but whatever comes of them, I know the fog will still roll in, the geese will come back every year, and as I awake at each daybreak, I'll be thankful that my passion for quilting remains.

Perhaps, metaphorically, this is why the Mariner's Compass is still my favorite block. Just as it has for sailors at sea, this navigational aide has provided me direction, inspiration, and comfort from the storm. It points in every direction: I (and you) have only to choose a path, stay the course, and it will lead safely toward new techniques, colors, and block ideas that will remain to enhance future quilting voyages. With a decade passed since I first wrote on this topic, I knew it was time to revisit and update this queen of blocks with all the new lessons I have learned. The results are in the pages that follow.

M'Liss

Mariner's Compass
and Medallion Quilts:
A PLACE IN HISTORY

The Mariner's Medallion quilts featured in this book are a combination of two time-honored traditions in American quiltmaking: the Mariner's Compass block, consisting of a circular pattern with a series of radiating points, and the medallion-style quilt, traditionally composed of a singular central motif framed by a series of pieced, appliquéd, and/or unpieced borders.

The Mariner's Compass motif has long been associated with the wind or compass roses found on maritime maps and charts. The design first appeared in patchwork in an English quilt ascribed to the first half of the eighteenth century; the first American example dates to the 1830s.

While the Mariner's Compass can be found in block-style quilts dating from around 1825, it made its earliest appearance in the medallion format. The intricate piecework, the exciting potential for achieving three-dimensional effects, and the dramatic tension of the multiple radiating points made the Mariner's Compass—then, as now—a natural for the dramatic, center-stage treatment of the medallion style.

Some of the oldest surviving quilts from both Europe and America are medallion quilts. Early examples included heavily quilted, largely wholecloth quilts, with sunbursts and stars as common central themes. In time, printed panels were imported and then manufactured especially for use as the central motifs in these stunning quilts. In other examples, exquisite (and expensive!) chintz fabrics were purchased, and their large motifs were carefully cut and appliquéd whole, using a technique called *broderie perse*. Quilters used the precious leftovers judiciously for pieced and appliquéd border motifs. One notable figure to whom early medallion-style quilts have been attributed is Martha Washington, wife of our nation's first president.

As the Civil War approached, album and block-style quilts usurped the medallion quilt from its popular position, but such an elegant and classic genre was not to vanish forever. Rediscovered by quiltmakers in the 1920s and 1930s in the form of realistic floral appliqué designs, the medallion quilt experienced yet another renaissance in the last quarter of the twentieth century—a love affair that continues to this day.

Today's medallion quilts are as unique as their makers, and the Mariner's Medallion quilts in these pages are no exception. Trust me: Once you have made one of these fabulous quilts, you will undoubtedly want to make another. In doing so, you will simultaneously honor and advance the history of this venerable art form.

TOOLS AND NOTIONS

Good news! You don't need a lot of fancy gadgets or special equipment to make a Mariner's Medallion quilt. The basics—with a few easy-to-find additions—work perfectly. Here is a list of what you'll need, with thoughts about my personal favorite features:

Rotary cutter: with an ergonomic-style grip and a reliable safety catch

Cutting mat: green, with a grid (Lines marking the 45° angle are helpful.)

Acrylic rulers: both the 6″ × 24″ and 6″ × 12″ sizes, preferably with the 45° angle indicated

Ruler grips: the clear type. These adhesive tabs stick to the bottom of your rulers and keep them from slipping as you cut.

Pins: Fine, glass-head silk pins don't leave unsightly holes in the fabric. (**Note:** We used larger, quilter-type pins in the how-to photos so the pins would be more visible.)

Scissors: fabric scissors, paper-cutting scissors, and small embroidery-type scissors for cutting thread

Seam ripper: with an ergonomic-style handle

Thread: 100% cotton thread in a neutral color for piecing; thread in a contrasting color for basting the compass to the compass background square; and thread to match the compass background for appliqué

Paper for foundation piecing: for the compasses and some of the blocks in the Block Gallery (pages 20–34). Choose something that you can see through well enough to place the fabric pieces and that will tear away easily when sewing is complete. There are several products, available at most quilt shops, designed and marketed specifically for this purpose. For example, *Simple Foundation Translucent Vellum Paper* (see Resources on page 72) is a good choice if you plan to hand trace the foundation patterns. Plain newsprint, tracing paper, or computer paper are other options for foundation piecing.

Tweezers: helpful for removing foundation papers

Temporary spray adhesive for fabric (optional): a suitable substitute for basting the completed compass to the compass background square (see page 14). One of my favorites is Sulky KK 2000 (see Resources on page 72).

Sewing machine: in good working order, with a ¼″ presser foot to help keep piecing accurate. If your machine does not come with this foot, I strongly recommend that you buy one!

Sewing machine needles: a good supply so you can change needles after each project

Additional sewing machine attachments: If you plan to machine quilt, a dual-feed or walking foot is a must for straight-line quilting and is also a great help when applying bindings. A darning foot is useful for free-motion quilting (see Quilting Your Quilt on page 68).

FABRIC

Because I'm a purist, I prefer to use 100% cotton fabrics in my quilts. It is soft, is easy to work with, wears well, and is very forgiving. In general, I stay away from polyester and polyester-cotton blends, which have a tendency to ravel and can be slippery and difficult to handle.

LAUNDRY DAY! Prewashing, a practice I advocate, will preshrink the fabric, remove any excess finishing chemicals and dyes, and make the fabric softer to the touch. I prewash all new fabric (fat quarters in the sink, ½ yard and larger pieces in the washing machine). Next comes the ironing: straight from the dryer, fabrics are ironed, squared up, and on the shelf in no time.

CHOOSING FABRIC

The projects in this book call for six fabrics for the compass (including the compass center and the compass background), a fabric for the compass background square, and yardages for plain (unpieced) borders, bindings, and backing. Fabric amounts for pieced borders, including border blocks, appear in the Block Gallery (pages 20–34) and in Beautiful Borders: Pieced and Plain (pages 35–42). All yardage amounts are based on a usable fabric width—after removing selvages and laundering—of 40″.

Mariner's Medallion quilts tell a story, and the story you wish to tell can have a considerable bearing on the fabrics you choose. I often suggest to my students that they select a theme—a holiday, season, memory, or special event—and use it to help guide them in their fabric choices. Of course, nautical or other water-related themes are natural choices for these quilts.

FABRIC COLLECTIONS! A fabric collection is a great way to go about selecting the fabrics for a quilt. The patterns are designed to harmonize, the colorways are coordinated, and the ultimate look is very together! Many of the quilts in this book were designed around specific fabric collections. For example, for Dream Guide (page 48), I chose fabrics from Kimono Art, a fabric collection I designed.

Once you have a starting point, you are ready to choose the fabrics to make your own personal Mariner's Medallion quilt. As a rule, a variety in prints (pattern and scale), color, and value (lights, mediums, and darks) will make your quilt more interesting.

COMPASS FABRIC

You'll need fabric for three different parts of the compass circle: the compass points, the compass background, and the compass center.

Compass Points

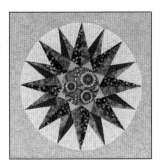

The compass in the Mariner's Medallion quilts features sixteen long points, divided into two categories of eight points each. The top points are split length-wise and are pieced from two different fabrics. The under points appear to sit behind the top points and, in most cases, are cut from a single piece of fabric, although these points can also be split, as demonstrated in Annette Barca's Our Garden in Autumn (page 64).

As you look through the quilts in this book, notice that the long points in most of the compasses vary in value from medium light to medium dark. While there is enough contrast to suggest a layered or three-dimensional effect, the contrast is not so strong that any one point demands attention.

"VALUE-ABLE" FABRIC! Value refers to the lightness or darkness of a color in relationship to those around it and is an essential factor in your quilt's success. Value creates contrast and allows you to see the pattern emerge. Even if you make a one-color quilt (also called monochromatic), the range from light to dark within that single color is what makes the quilt work.

In addition to the long top points and under points, there is a "crown" of points surrounding the center circle. Although these points are small, they play a powerful role by framing and showcasing the compass center. This is a good place for a bit of drama, such as an accent or "zinger" fabric like the bright orangey-gold I used in *Dream Guide* (page 48).

Compass Background

Compass background fabrics are often light in value to create contrast with the darker compass points. Many quilters choose neutral colors (e.g., white, ecru, gray, etc.) for their compass backgrounds, but I like to think that we can take liberty and add our own personal neutral colors to the standard list. Your neutral can simply be your favorite color in its lightest value.

Of course, using a light fabric for the background is not an absolute! You might prefer to go darker for your background. The strong red I used for the compass background in *The Garden Court Compass* (page 42) is a good example of how an unexpected choice can add excitement and visual power to a familiar motif. The main thing is to maintain a noticeable contrast between the background and the compass points.

At first glance, it might appear that the subtle geometric print Barbara Higbee-Price chose for her compass background in *Vintage Americana* (page 58) was an unusual decision. Yet considering her quilt's theme, it is the *perfect* choice.

Carla Zimmermann went a step further in choosing the compass background fabric for *Oriental Legends Whisper Beneath the Waves* (page 47). She used *two* prints of similar color and value instead of the single fabric most quilters select for this role … another example of the creative choices possible when you are willing to take a risk.

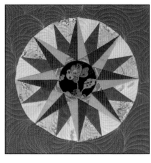

Compass Center

There are so many dramatic and creative options for this focal point, but don't get hung up now on choosing the perfect fabric for the center circle of your Mariner's Compass block. This is an important decision: The focal point of the Mariner's Compass block—and, therefore, your entire Mariner's Medallion quilt—is the center circle of the compass. Take time to let the quilt evolve. I often suggest waiting until the quilt top is complete before choosing the center circle. As you work, your quilt will take on a distinct personality. Let that personality develop; you might be surprised at some of the options it reveals along the way. Here are some ideas; details appear at the bottom of page 9.

Select a motif from your theme fabric and fussy cut a center circle, as Annette Barca did in *Mariner's Compass With Red Koi* (page 46).

Fussy cut a border striped fabric in wedges and repiece it for a kaleidoscopic effect, as Marie L. Miller did in *Queen Isabel's Pillow* (page 43).

Create and appliqué a motif, as Susie Kincy did in *Look What M'Liss Started* (page 64).

Appliqué a purchased motif, as I did in *Viva Las Vegas* (page 44).

Embroider the center circle with a theme-related motif, as I did in *Voices From My Garden* (page 53).

Transfer a favorite photograph to fabric, as John and Louise James did for *Northwest Compass* (page 63).

Just use your imagination. I have no doubt you'll come up with something wonderful!

COMPASS BACKGROUND SQUARE

Your choice of fabric here will depend largely upon the effect you desire for the compass itself. If you want the compass points to really pop and for the compass to appear as if it's floating on the background, use the

same fabric for the compass background square as you use for the compass background. This is the approach Carla Zimmermann used in *The Mariner's Favorite Stowaway* (page 47). Set against a unified, crisp white background, the deep red and indigo compass points seem to burst from the quilt's center.

If you prefer to see your compass framed as a centerpiece, select a fabric different from the one you use for the compass background. Depending on the amount of contrast in color, value, or visual texture, the framing effect can be dramatic, as in my quilt *Viva Las Vegas* (page 44), or more subtle, as in Vicki DeGraaf's *Summer Sunsets* (page 51).

BORDER FABRICS

Large-scale prints make great outer borders for Mariner's Medallion quilts—as you can see from many of the quilts in this book! You'll need to plan ahead, though. Some large-scale prints are pictorial and/or directional, so they might require extra yardage, as well as extra time and effort in planning and cutting. Whatever your decision, you'll want to choose border fabrics that complement and enhance your design, rather than overpower it.

There are many other options for selecting an appropriate border fabric:

- Misunderstood, overlooked, and often underused, striped fabrics make fabulous borders, especially inner borders. See for yourself in *I'd Rather Be Sailing* (page 52).

- If your quilt features a wide range of prints and/or colors, a multicolored paisley or floral can tie them together. *Summer Sunsets* (page 51) and *Our Garden in Autumn* (page 64) are good examples.

- *Viva Las Vegas* (page 44), *My Beautiful Balloon* (page 51), and *Land of Liberty* (page 62) all demonstrate the success of a border fabric chosen to reflect the quilt's theme.

Now that you've started, you'll no doubt come up with many of your own creative fabric solutions.

Mariner's Compass With Red Koi

Queen Isabel's Pillow

Look What M'Liss Started

Viva Las Vegas

Voices From My Garden

Northwest Compass

Making the
MARINER'S COMPASS BLOCK

he centerpiece of your Mariner's Medallion quilt is—of course—the Mariner's Compass block. This chapter covers my simple Foundation Piecing method for achieving accurate, dramatic compass designs. It also gives you the full-size wedge and center circle patterns for the compass in two sizes: 16½" diameter (pages 72–73; fits a 19" × 19" or larger finished square) and 11" diameter (pages 72–73; fits a 12" × 12" or larger finished square). The larger version is used to complete the Mariner's Medallion Wallhanging (page 44), the Mariner's Medallion Lap Quilt (page 48), and the Mariner's Medallion Full-Size Quilt (page 59). The smaller version is used for the Mariner's Medallion On Point (page 53).

Construction is the same regardless of the size compass (and block) you are making. Only the sizes of the pieces will change.

GUIDELINES FOR FOUNDATION PIECING

Here are some simple guidelines to launch you on a successful foundation-piecing experience.

■ Make the required number of patterns or pattern units for the block you have chosen. If you are using a photocopier, make all copies on the same machine to ensure consistency.

■ Set your sewing machine to a smaller-than-usual stitch length (i.e., 1.5 or 16–20 stitches per inch). This will make it easier to remove the foundations later.

■ When placing the fabric shapes (and when stitching), hold the foundation printed side up. Always hold the foundation the same way. This will help you avoid placing (and sewing!) the wrong fabric shape in the wrong area.

■ Position the fabric shapes on the blank side of the foundation, so the fabric edges extend at least ¼" beyond the appropriate stitching line. This is essential; hold the unit up to a light source if necessary to assist you with fabric placement.

■ Stitch directly on the line, beginning ¼" from the inside edge of the foundation and stitching from the inner to the outer edge of the unit. Backstitch at the outer edge of the fabric and continue stitching ¼" beyond the edge of the foundation.

■ As you add each new fabric shape, trim the seam allowance to ¼" between the pieces. Trim the excess fabric ½" to ¾" beyond the edge of the foundation.

■ Gently press the seamline to set the stitches before opening each newly added fabric shape.

MATERIALS

All yardage is based on fabric that is 40" wide after laundering, unless noted otherwise.

16½" COMPASS

⅓ yard *each* of 5 different fabrics for center and points

½ yard fabric for background

11" COMPASS

¼ yard *each* of 5 different fabrics for center and points

⅓ yard fabric for background

CUTTING

Cut all strips across the fabric width. Patterns for the center circles are on page 74.

16½"-DIAMETER COMPASS
From Fabric A:
Cut 2 strips 2¾" × 40".

From Fabric B:
Cut 3 strips 4" × 40".

From *each* of Fabrics C and D:

Cut 2 strips 2½″ × 40″ (4 total).

From Fabric E:

Cut 1 strip 2½″ × 40″.

From Fabric F:

Cut 1 large center circle.

11″-DIAMETER COMPASS

From Fabric A:

Cut 1 strip 2½″ × 40″.

From Fabric B:

Cut 2 strips 3″ × 40″.

From *each* of Fabrics C and D:

Cut 2 strips 2″ × 40″ (4 total).

From Fabric E:

Cut 1 strip 2″ × 40″.

From Fabric F:

Cut 1 small center circle.

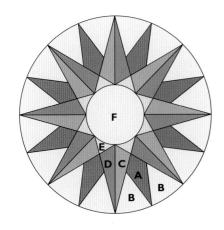

MAKING THE WEDGES

The foundation patterns for the 16½″ compass wedge and the 11″ compass wedge are on page 73. Before you begin, trace or photocopy eight foundations for the size compass you are making. (See page 6 for suggestions on appropriate foundation materials.) Cut out each foundation directly on the outermost line.

1. Turn the paper foundation printed side up. On the blank side of the foundation, place fabric pieces 1 and 2 right sides together so they completely cover the area marked 1, extending at least ¼″ beyond the marked seamlines. Pin.

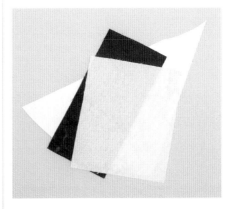

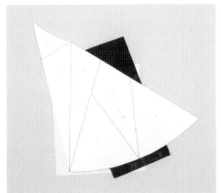

2. Stitch directly on the line between the areas marked 1 and 2 on the foundation. Finish with a backstitch.

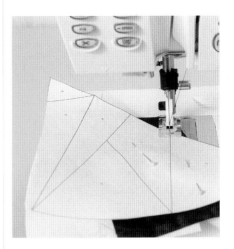

3. Turn over the foundation, open fabric piece 2, and press toward the area marked 2. Trim the seam allowance between pieces 1 and 2 to ¼″.

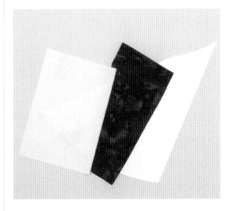

4. Once again, turn the paper foundation printed side up. On the blank side of the foundation, place fabric piece 3 right sides together with fabric piece 1 so the edges of piece 3 extend at least ¼″ beyond the marked seamlines. Stitch directly on the line between the areas marked 1 and 3 on the foundation. Finish with a backstitch. Open and press fabric piece 3. Trim the seam allowance between pieces 1 and 3 to ¼″.

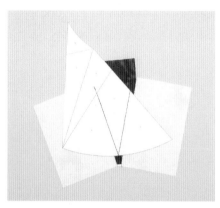

5. Repeat to position fabric piece 4 over fabric pieces 1/3. Stitch directly on the line between the areas marked 4 and 1/3. Open and press fabric piece 4. Trim the seam allowance between pieces 1/3 and 4 to ¼″.

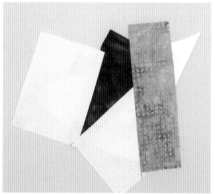

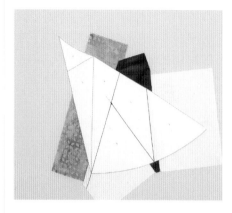

6. Repeat to position fabric piece 5 over fabric piece 4. Stitch directly on the line between the areas marked 5 and 4. Open and press fabric piece 5. Trim the seam allowance between pieces 4 and 5 to ¼″.

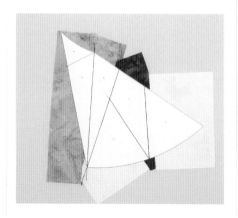

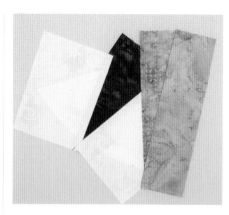

7. Repeat to position fabric piece 6 over fabric piece 5. Stitch directly on the line between the areas marked 6 and 5. Open and press fabric piece 6. Trim the seam allowance between pieces 5 and 6 to ¼″.

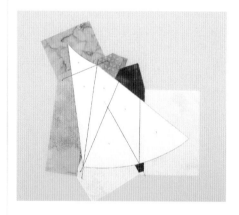

8. With the stitched foundation printed side up, trim the excess fabric ¼″ from the outer edge of the foundation pattern.

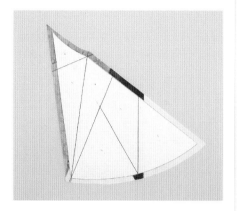

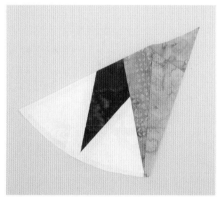

9. Repeat Steps 1–8 to make a total of 8 wedges, chain piecing them if you wish.

ASSEMBLING THE COMPASS

Before you begin, arrange the eight foundation-pieced wedges in a circle to form the compass. Refer to the photo at right for guidance.

1. Place 2 adjacent wedges right sides together and, with raw edges aligned, carefully match the seams of fabric pieces 1/4 on one wedge with the seams of fabric pieces 5/6 on the other wedge. Pin the intersection first and

then add more pins to secure the wedges. Sew the wedges together right along the edges of the foundation patterns. Make 4 pairs.

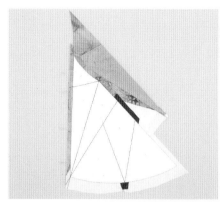

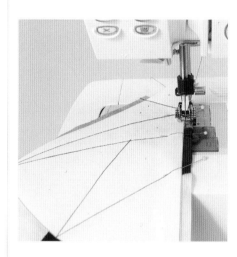

2. Join 2 pairs from Step 1 to make compass halves. Make 2. Sew the halves together to complete the outer compass. Carefully press the seams in one direction.

3. Machine sew a basting stitch all around the outer compass edge, right along the foundation edge. Working with the paper side up, carefully press a ¼″ seam allowance to the paper side of the compass. Press the compass from the front side and carefully remove the paper foundations.

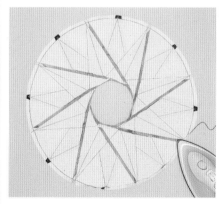

PAPER, BE GONE! Keep a seam ripper and a spray mister filled with water on hand for removing the foundations. A fine mist will soften the paper, and you can use the seam ripper to carefully nudge the damp foundation away from any stubborn seams.

4. Press the background square, using a touch of starch if you wish. Moving from the center outward, carefully finger-press the square in half vertically and then horizontally. Open the square and use the finger-pressed guidelines to center the compass on the square. You can center either the larger split points or the under points of the compass. Centering the under points emphasizes the small triangles around the center circle.

5. Taking care not to shift or distort the circle, secure the compass to the background square by pinning around the outside edges of the compass. Beginning at the inside edge, use thread in a contrasting color to hand baste the compass to the square in concentric circles. Space the basting lines 1″–2″ apart, removing the pins as you come to them.

SKIP THE STITCHES! If you prefer, use a temporary fabric adhesive spray, such as Sulky KK 2000 (see Resources on page 72), instead of basting, to hold the compass in place.

6. Use thread that matches the compass background to hand appliqué the compass to the background square. Use a seam ripper to carefully remove any basting stitches from Step 3 that are visible around the compass perimeter. Leave the concentric basting lines in place for now.

ADDING THE CENTER CIRCLE

1. Use the appropriately sized pattern (page 74) to make a template. Cut the center circle for your Mariner's Compass. You do not need to add a seam allowance; a ¼″ seam allowance is already included in the pattern.

2. Using your ¼″ foot as a guide and a slightly longer-than-usual stitch length, machine stitch ¼″ from the raw edge all around the perimeter of the fabric circle. Clip the thread, leaving a nice long tail.

3. Gently pull one of the thread tails just enough so the edges of the circle turn under, creating a ¼″ seam allowance. Carefully press the newly turned edge.

Compass Pillow, 18″ round, made by Peggy J. Johnson, 2005.

4. Fold and finger-press the center circle both vertically and horizontally to find its center. Place the circle on the Mariner's Compass block, carefully considering any directional fabric or embroidery motifs. Pin the circle to the block, matching the edge of the circle with the seam points of Fabric E (area 6) on the compass. Add additional pins as needed.

Traveling Mariner's Compass (vest), made by Peggy J. Johnson, 2005.

5. Use a blind stitch and matching thread to hand stitch the circle to the block. Remove the basting and press. If the background fabric behind the compass or compass center is dark enough to shadow through, I cut it away, leaving a ¼″ seam allowance. Otherwise, I leave it in place as a "stabilizer."

Traveling Mariner's Compass, back view.

A BOUNTY OF BLOCKS

ere's a specially selected collection of blocks to launch your creative journey. Use these blocks to duplicate the project quilts or as a springboard to a quilt of your own design. Add fabric, thread, out-of-the-ordinary quilting motifs, embroidery, and embellishment, and you are on your way.

There are 30 blocks or block units given alphabetically in the Block Gallery (pages 20–34), with some in multiple sizes, giving you loads of flexibility. To help you out, I've indexed them here according to size.

Cutting instructions yield one block. For blocks given in multiple sizes, construction is the same, regardless of the block size. Susie Kincy, John James, and my sister, Erin Rae Vautier, helped me piece the blocks.

Don't feel restricted by the blocks you see here. Check your favorite quilt books and magazines for other block options. C&T Publishing's *Quick & Easy Block Tool* is a fabulous source, presenting more than 100 blocks in a variety of sizes, all designed for rotary cutting (see Resources on page 72).

BLOCK INDEX (BY SIZE)

4″ blocks: Broken Dishes, Double Bluff, Four-Patch, Wild Waves

6″ blocks: Arctic Nights, Attic Window, Chinese Junk, Cry of the Loon, Evergreen Tree, Fish, Great Blue Heron, Log Cabin, Ohio Star, Sail Away, Sailboat, Sawtooth Star, Sunrise, Tall Ship, Topiary Trio, Wild Waves

7″ blocks: Arctic Nights, Mariner's Embroidery, Ocean Wave, Port and Starboard, Whirlpool

Odd-Sized Blocks and Units

2″ × 4″ units: Flying Geese, Honeycomb

6″ × 5″ block: Lodgepole Pines

6″ × 6¼″ block: Filbert Tree

6″ × 6½″ block: Douglas Fir Tree

6″ × 9¾″ block: Coast Guard House

6″ × 12¼″ block: Lighthouse

Blocks and Units in Multiple Sizes

Arctic Nights, Wild Waves

TIME-SAVING TIPS AND TECHNIQUES

The following quick-cutting, easy-piecing, and no-fuss appliqué methods will save you time and/or improve your accuracy as you assemble the blocks in the Block Gallery.

ROTARY CUTTING

A great many pieces for the blocks (and borders) for the quilts in this book can be cut with a rotary cutter. Make sure that the fabric is pressed and that you fold it carefully before cutting. **Note:** Cutting instructions are for right-handers. Reverse if you are left-handed.

Cutting Strips and Pieces

Use your ruler, not the markings on the mat, to measure and cut strips and pieces. I use the grid on my mat for aligning the fabric and for taking general measurements, not for making precise measurements. Square the raw edges of the fabric before you begin.

1. Working with the fabric's squared left edge, use your ruler to measure and cut a strip of the desired width. Repeat to cut the required number of strips. Be sure to square up the edge of the fabric after every few cuts.

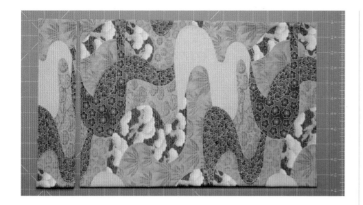

2. Cut the strip into squares or other smaller segments as directed in the project instructions.

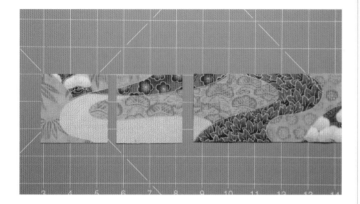

SEAM ALLOWANCES AND PRESSING

Unless otherwise noted, you'll be using a ¼″ seam allowance for piecing the blocks in the Block Gallery. Before you begin to sew, it's a good idea to stitch a test piece to check that your ¼″ seam is accurate.

The construction process is simple: you'll sew pieces into units, units into rows or sections, and rows or sections together to complete the block or the quilt. The project instructions will tell you which way to press the seams, either in the step itself or with arrows in the accompanying diagrams.

For the blocks, or when in doubt, follow these general guidelines:

■ Press toward the darker fabric when possible.

■ Press in opposite directions from row to row. This helps your seams match evenly and lie flat.

FLIP AND SEW

You'll love this quick-and-easy piecing method! Using only squares and rectangles, you'll achieve perfect little triangles on such blocks as Filbert Tree (page 24), Flying Geese (page 25), Honeycomb (page 27), and Tall Ship (page 33).

1. Use a ruler and marking tool to draw a diagonal line from corner to corner on the wrong side of each small square, as indicated in the block diagram for the block you are making.

2. With raw edges aligned, place the small marked squares right sides together with the larger square or rectangle, as indicated in the block diagram. Sew directly on the diagonal lines.

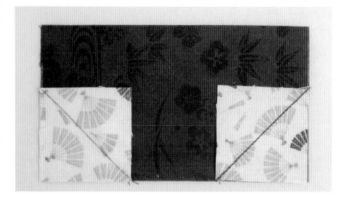

3. Cut away the excess fabric, leaving a ¼″ seam allowance. Press the seams toward the small squares.

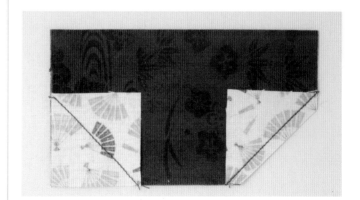

4. Repeat Steps 2 and 3 to add additional squares as needed.

FOUNDATION PIECING

Five blocks in the Block Gallery—Chinese Junk (page 21), Lodgepole Pines (page 28), Sailboat (page 31), Sunrise (page 32), and Topiary Trio (page 33)—are all or partially foundation-pieced. The process is the same as that used for piecing the wedges of the Mariner's Compass blocks (pages 11–13).

FUSIBLE APPLIQUÉ

Try this quick-and-easy method for adding appliqués to Coast Guard House (page 22) and Lighthouse (page 27). Normally you would reverse the patterns for fusible appliqué, but the appliqué pieces in these blocks are symmetrical—that is, the left and right sides are mirror images—so there is no need to reverse them.

1. Trace the appliqué shape directly on the paper side of the fusible web. Rough cut the paper pattern, leaving a margin of paper around the traced motif.

2. Following the manufacturer's instructions for heat setting and pressing times, iron the fusible pattern web side down to the wrong side of the appliqué fabric.

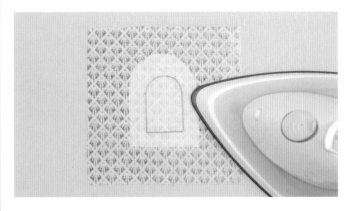

3. Cut out the fabric shape directly on the traced line.

4. Remove the paper backing and fuse the shape to the block. Finish the edges with machine blanket, satin, or other decorative stitching.

STRIP PIECING

Douglas Fir Tree (page 23), Evergreen Tree (page 24), Filbert Tree (page 24), and Lodgepole Pines (page 28) include strip-pieced areas. The process is the same as that used for piecing the Bargello border (page 38).

MITERED CORNERS

The Attic Window block (page 20) includes two strips of differing value that are mitered at the corner of a square to form a shaded, three-dimensional effect. Follow these easy steps to achieve a neat, accurate miter.

1. Begin with the left A strip. With right sides together, align the edge of the A strip with the upper left edge of the B square; sew the strip to the square. Stop stitching and take a backstitch ¼" from the edge of the square where the miter will be. Press the seam toward the strip.

2. With right sides together, align the edge of the remaining A strip with the lower right edge of the B square; sew the strip to the square. Stop stitching and take a backstitch at the point where the stitching meets the seam from Step 1. Press the seam toward the strip.

3. Place the block right side up on your ironing board. Place the unstitched "tail" of one A strip on top of the adjacent strip. Fold under the top strip at a 45° angle so it aligns with the edge of the strip underneath. Press the fold lightly. Use a ruler or right angle to be certain the angle is correct and the corner is square. Press again, firmly.

4. Fold the block diagonally, right sides together, aligning the 45° pressing marks and the long edges of the strips. Place pins near the pressed fold to secure the strip corners for sewing. Begin with a backstitch at the seam at

Stitch toward outside edge.

the miter's inside corner and then carefully stitch toward the outside edge along the fold. Finish with a backstitch.

5. Trim the excess strip fabric, leaving a ¼" seam allowance; press the seam open.

BLOCK GALLERY

ARCTIC NIGHTS
6", 7"

CUTTING

6" Block

From *each* **of Fabrics 1 and 2:**

Cut 4 squares $1\frac{1}{4}$" × $1\frac{1}{4}$" (A1 and A2).

Cut 2 rectangles $1\frac{1}{4}$" × 2" (B1 and B2).

Cut 2 squares 2" × 2" (C1 and C2).

Cut 2 rectangles 2" × $3\frac{1}{2}$" (D1 and D2).

7" Block

From *each* **of Fabrics 1 and 2:**

Cut 4 squares $1\frac{3}{8}$" × $1\frac{3}{8}$" (A1 and A2).

Cut 2 rectangles $1\frac{3}{8}$" × $2\frac{1}{4}$" (B1 and B2).

Cut 2 squares $2\frac{1}{4}$" × $2\frac{1}{4}$" (C1 and C2).

Cut 2 rectangles $2\frac{1}{4}$" × 4" (D1 and D2).

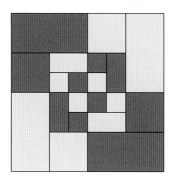

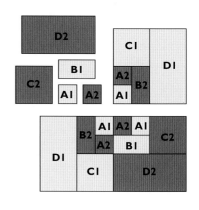

ATTIC WINDOW
6"

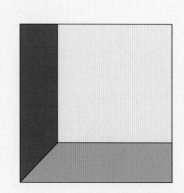

CUTTING

From *each* **of Fabrics 1 and 2:**
Cut 1 rectangle 2" × 7" (A1 and A2).

From Fabric 3:
Cut 1 square 5" × 5" (B).

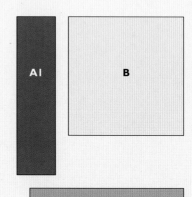

CUTTING

From *each* of Fabrics 1–4:

Cut 1 square 2⅞" × 2⅞"; cut once diagonally to yield 2 half-square triangles (A1, A2, A3, and A4).

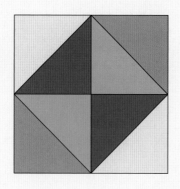

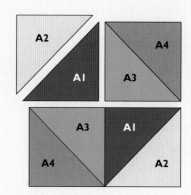

CUTTING

From Fabric 1:

Cut 1 square 3" × 3" (A).

Cut 1 square 4½" × 4½" (C).

Cut 1 rectangle 2" × 2½" (H).

Cut 1 square 2" × 1½" (I).

Cut 1 rectangle 2¼" × 4¾" (J).

Cut 1 rectangle 1⅜" × 5⅝" (K).

From Fabric 2:

Cut 1 rectangle 4½" × 6" (B).

From Fabric 3:

Cut 1 rectangle 2" × 5" (D).

Cut 1 square 2" × 2" (G).

From Fabric 4:

Cut 1 rectangle 2" × 4" (E).

Cut 1 rectangle 2" × 2½" (F).

Assemble the sailboat portions of this block (sail, boat, and prow) using the Foundation Piecing method (page 10). The foundation patterns are on page 75. Note that pieces A–I are cut oversize for the Foundation Piecing method.

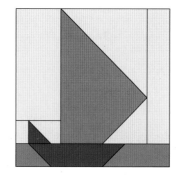

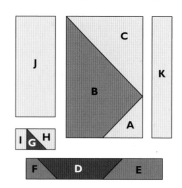

CUTTING

From *each* of Fabrics 1 and 2:
Cut 1 square 3⅞" × 3⅞" (A); cut once diagonally to yield 2 half-square triangles (A1 and A2).

From Fabric 3:
Cut 1 rectangle 1" × 2" (B).

From Fabric 4:
Cut 1 rectangle 1" × 6½" (C).

From Fabric 5:
Cut 2 rectangles 1½" × 6½" (D).
Cut 2 rectangles 1¼" × 2¾" (E).
Cut 2 rectangles 1½" × 1¾" (G).
Cut 2 rectangles 1" × 2¾" (I).

From Fabric 6:
Cut 1 rectangle 2" × 2¾" (F).

From Fabric 7:
Cut 2 squares 1½" × 1½" (H).

From each of Fabrics 8 and 9:
Cut 1 rectangle 1½" × 6½" (J and K).

Once you've decided where to place the chimney, trim the bottom edge at a 45° angle, fuse it in place, and finish with invisible or decorative machine stitching (page 18).

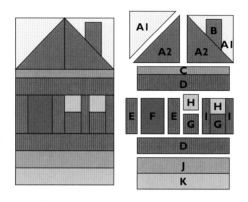

CUTTING

From Fabric 1:
Cut 1 square 3¼" × 3¼"; cut twice diagonally to yield 4 quarter-square triangles (A1).

Cut 2 squares 2⅞" × 2⅞"; cut each square once diagonally to yield 2 half-square triangles (4 total) (B1).

Cut 1 square 2½" × 2½" (C).

From Fabric 2:
Cut 1 square 3¼" × 3¼"; cut twice diagonally to yield 4 quarter-square triangles (A2).

Cut 2 squares 2⅞" × 2⅞"; cut each square once diagonally to yield 2 half-square triangles (4 total) (B2).

From Fabric 3:
Cut 2 squares 2⅞" × 2⅞"; cut each square once diagonally to yield 2 half-square triangles (4 total) (B3).

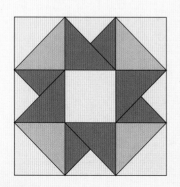
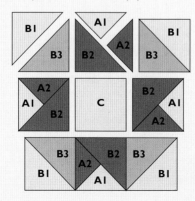

CUTTING

From *each* of Fabrics 1 and 2:
Cut 1 square $2\frac{7}{8}" \times 2\frac{7}{8}"$; cut once diagonally to yield 2 half-square triangles (A1 and A2).

From Fabric 3:
Cut 2 squares $2\frac{1}{2}" \times 2\frac{1}{2}"$ (B).

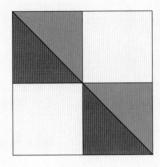

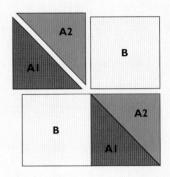

DOUGLAS FIR TREE

6" X 6½"

CUTTING

Patterns for A and B are on page 77.

From the strip-pieced unit:
Cut 3 A.

From Fabric 1:
Cut 3 *each* of B and B reverse.
Cut 2 rectangles $1\frac{3}{4}" \times 3\frac{1}{8}"$ (C).

From Fabric 2:
Cut 1 rectangle $1\frac{1}{4}" \times 1\frac{3}{4}"$ (D).

Assemble the treetop portions of this block (A) using the Strip Piecing technique (page 38). Begin by strip piecing random-width strips to make a strip-pieced unit that measures approximately 8" × 8".

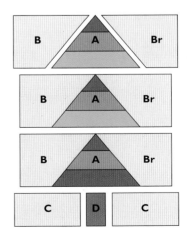

CUTTING

Patterns for A–F are on page 76.

From the strip-pieced unit:
Cut 1 *each* of A, C, and E.

From Fabric 1:
Cut 1 *each* of B and B reverse, D and D reverse, and F and F reverse.

Cut 2 rectangles 1½" × 3" (G).

From Fabric 2:
Cut 1 square 1½" × 1½" (H).

Assemble the treetop portions of this block (A, C, and E) using the Strip Piecing technique (page 38). Begin by strip piecing random-width strips to make a strip-pieced unit that measures approximately 8" × 8".

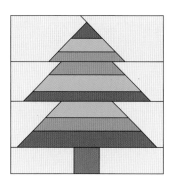

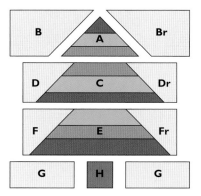

CUTTING

From the strip-pieced unit:
Cut 1 rectangle 5½" × 4¾" (B).

From Fabric 1:
Cut 4 squares 1¾" × 1¾" (A).

Cut 2 rectangles 1" × 4¾" (C).

Cut 1 rectangle 1¼" × 6½" (D).

Cut 2 rectangles 1¾" × 3" (E).

From Fabric 2:
Cut 1 rectangle 1½" × 1¾" (F).

Assemble the treetop portion of this block (B) using the Strip Piecing technique (page 38). Begin by strip piecing random-width strips to make a strip-pieced unit that measures approximately 6" × 6". Assemble the block using the Flip and Sew method (page 17).

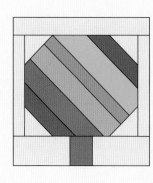

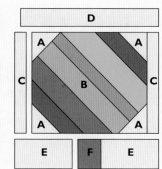

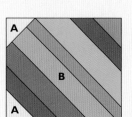

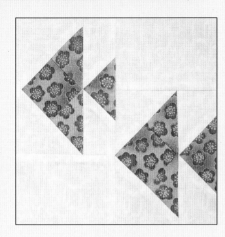

CUTTING

Pattern for D is on page 75.

From Fabric 1:

Cut 2 squares 2⅞" × 2⅞"; cut each square once diagonally to yield 2 half-square triangles (4 total) (C).

Cut 2 D and 2 D reverse.

Cut 2 rectangles 2½" × 3½" (E).

From Fabric 2:

Cut 2 squares 1⅞" × 1⅞" (A).

Cut 2 squares 3¼" × 3¼"; cut twice diagonally to yield 4 quarter-square triangles (8 total) (B). You will have 2 triangles left over.

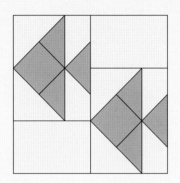

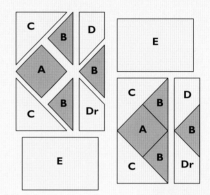

Assemble this block using the Flip and Sew method (page 17).

CUTTING

From Fabric 1:
Cut 2 squares 2½" × 2½" (A).

From Fabric 2:
Cut 1 rectangle 2½" × 4½" (B).

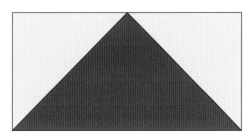

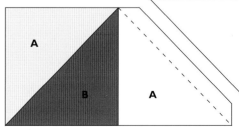

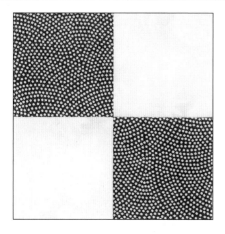

CUTTING

From *each* of Fabrics 1 and 2:

Cut 2 squares 2½" × 2½" (A1 and A2).

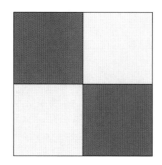

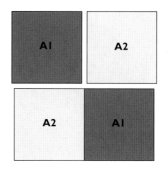

GREAT BLUE HERON

6"

CUTTING

From Fabric 1:

Cut 4 squares 2⅞" × 2⅞"; cut each square once diagonally to yield 2 half-square triangles (8 total) (A1). You will have 1 triangle left over.

From Fabric 2:

Cut 3 squares 2⅞" × 2⅞"; cut each square once diagonally to yield 2

half-square triangles (6 total) (A2). You will have 1 triangle left over.

From Fabric 3:

Cut 1 square 2½" × 2½" (B).

Cut 1 square 4⅞" × 4⅞"; cut once diagonally to yield 2 half-square triangles (C). You will have 1 triangle left over.

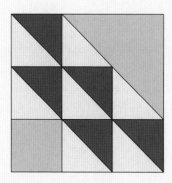

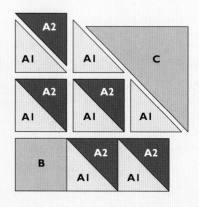

Assemble this block using the Flip and Sew method (page 17).

CUTTING

From Fabric 1:
Cut 4 squares 1½" × 1½" (A).

From Fabric 2:
Cut 1 rectangle 2½" × 4½" (B).

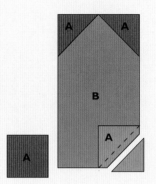

CUTTING

Patterns for A, B, E, and G are on page 78.

From Fabric 1:
Cut 1 *each* of A and A reverse.

Cut 2 rectangles 2" × 2¼" (C).

Cut 1 rectangle 6½" × 8" (F).

From Fabric 2:
Cut 1 B.

From Fabric 3:
Cut 1 rectangle 2" × 3" (D).

From Fabric 4:
Cut 1 E.

From Fabric 5:
Cut 2 G.

From Fabric 6:
Cut 1 rectangle 1¼" × 2" (H).

From *each* of Fabrics 7 and 8:
Cut 1 rectangle 1¼" × 6½" (I and J).

Use your preferred method to appliqué pieces E, G, and H to the block. If you prefer hand appliqué, add a ¼" seam allowance when you cut the appliqué shapes. For fusing (page 18), cut the shapes to the size of the pattern and finish the edges with decorative machine stitching.

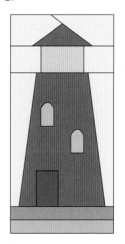
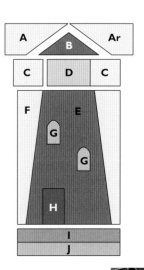

Note that pieces A, B, C, F, G, and H are cut oversize for the Foundation Piecing method.

CUTTING

From the strip-pieced unit:

Cut 1 rectangle 4" × 5" (A).

Cut 1 rectangle 4" × 4½" (F).

From Fabric 1:

Cut 2 rectangles 2½" × 5" (B and C).

Cut 2 rectangles 1½" × 1⅝" (D).

Cut 2 rectangles 2½" × 4½" (G and H).

Cut 2 rectangles 1¼" × 1⅝" (I).

Cut 1 rectangle 1½" × 3½" (K).

From Fabric 2:

Cut 1 rectangle 1¼" × 1½" (E).

Cut 1 square 1¼" × 1¼" (J).

Assemble the treetop portions of this block (A and F) using a combination of the Foundation Piecing method (page 10) and the Strip Piecing technique (page 38). Begin by strip piecing random-width strips to make a strip-pieced unit that measures approximately 8" × 10". The foundation patterns are on page 75.

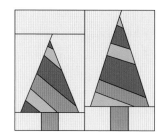

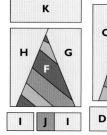

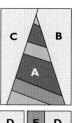

CUTTING

From Fabric 1:

Cut 1 square 2½" × 2½" (A).

From Fabric 2:

Cut 1 rectangle 1½" × 2½" (B).

Cut 1 rectangle 1½" × 4½" (D2).

From Fabric 3:

Cut 2 rectangles 1½" × 3½" (C).

From Fabric 4:

Cut 1 rectangle 1½" × 4½" (D4).

Cut 1 rectangle 1½" × 6½" (F).

From Fabric 5:

Cut 2 rectangles 1½" × 5½" (E).

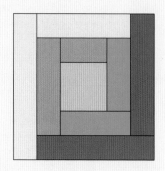

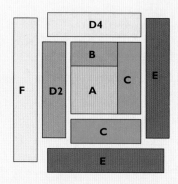

CUTTING

From Fabric 1:

Cut 1 square 5″ × 5″ (A).

From *each* of Fabrics 2 and 3:

Cut 2 strips $1\frac{3}{4}$″ × $6\frac{1}{4}$″
(B2 and B3).

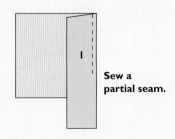

**Sew a
partial seam.**

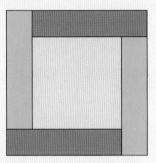

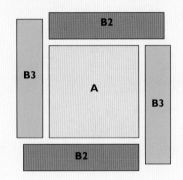

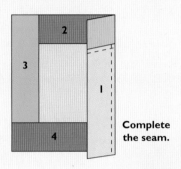

**Complete
the seam.**

OCEAN WAVE

7"

CUTTING

From Fabric 1:

Cut 5 squares $2\frac{5}{8}$″ × $2\frac{5}{8}$″; cut each
square once diagonally to yield 2
half-square triangles (10 total) (A1).

Cut 1 square $6\frac{1}{8}$″ × $6\frac{1}{8}$″; cut once
diagonally to yield 2 half-square
triangles (B1). You will have 1 triangle
left over.

From Fabric 2:

Cut 2 squares $2\frac{5}{8}$″ × $2\frac{5}{8}$″; cut each
square once diagonally to yield 2
half-square triangles (4 total) (A2).

From Fabric 3:

Cut 1 square $6\frac{1}{8}$″ × $6\frac{1}{8}$″; cut once
diagonally to yield 2 half-square triangles
(B3). You will have 1 triangle left over.

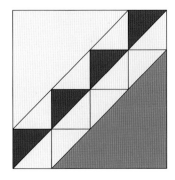

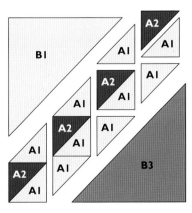

CUTTING

From Fabric 1:

Cut 1 square 3¼" × 3¼"; cut twice diagonally to yield 4 quarter-square triangles (A1).

Cut 4 squares 2½" × 2½" (B1).

From Fabric 2:

Cut 2 squares 3¼" × 3¼"; cut each square twice diagonally to yield 4 quarter-square triangles (8 total) (A2).

From Fabric 3:

Cut 1 square 3¼" × 3¼"; cut twice diagonally to yield 4 quarter-square triangles (A3).

From Fabric 4:

Cut 1 square 2½" × 2½" (B4).

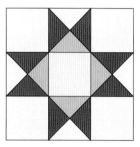

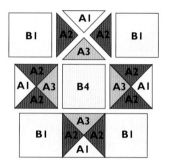

CUTTING

From Fabric 1:

Cut 8 squares 2⅝" × 2⅝"; cut each square once diagonally to yield 2 half-square triangles (16 total) (A1).

From *each* of Fabrics 2 and 3:

Cut 4 squares 2⅝" × 2⅝"; cut each square once diagonally to yield 2 half-square triangles (8 total from each fabric) (A2 and A3).

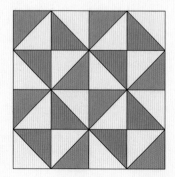

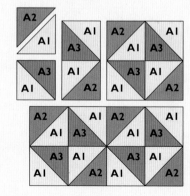

CUTTING

From Fabric 1:

Cut 2 squares 3¼" × 3¼"; cut each square twice diagonally to yield 4 quarter-square triangles (8 total) (A1). You will have 2 triangles left over.

Cut 1 square 3⅞" × 3⅞"; cut once diagonally to yield 2 half-square triangles (B1).

From Fabric 2:

Cut 1 square 3¼" × 3¼"; cut twice diag-onally to yield 4 quarter-square triangles (A2). You will have 1 triangle left over.

From Fabric 3:

Cut 1 square 3⅞" × 3⅞"; cut once diagonally to yield 2 half-square triangles (B3).

Cut 1 square 7¼" × 7¼"; cut twice diagonally to yield 4 quarter-square triangles (C). You will have 3 triangles left over.

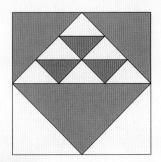

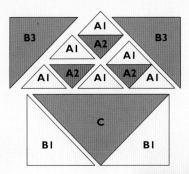

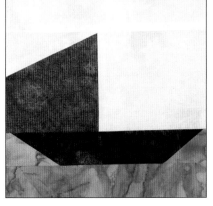

CUTTING

From Fabric 1:

Cut 1 square 4" × 4" (A).

Cut 1 rectangle 2" × 4" (C).

Cut 1 rectangle 1½" × 6½" (G1).

From Fabric 2:

Cut 1 square 4" × 4" (B).

From Fabric 3:

Cut 1 rectangle 2" × 7" (D).

From Fabric 4:

Cut 2 rectangles 2" × 3" (E and F).

Cut 1 rectangle 1½" × 6½" (G4).

Asssemble the sailboat portion of this block using the Foundation Piecing method (page 10). The foundation pattern is on page 74. Note that pieces A–F are cut oversize for the Foundation Piecing method.

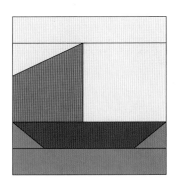

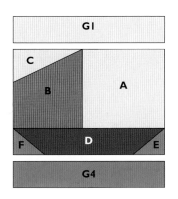

CUTTING

From Fabric 1:

Cut 4 squares 2⅜″ × 2⅜″; cut each square once diagonally to yield 2 half-square triangles (8 total) (A).

Cut 1 square 3½″ × 3½″ (D).

From Fabric 2:

Cut 1 square 4¼″ × 4¼″; cut twice diagonally to yield 4 quarter-square triangles (B).

Cut 4 squares 2″ × 2″ (C).

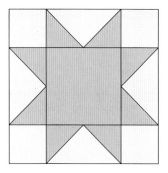

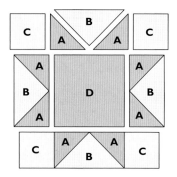

CUTTING

Pattern for H is on page 77.

From Fabric 1:

Cut 2 rectangles 2½″ × 5″ (A and G).

Cut 2 rectangles 2″ × 6″ (C and E).

From Fabric 2:

Cut 2 rectangles 2″ × 5″ (B and F).

Cut 1 rectangle 3″ × 7″ (D).

From Fabric 3:

Cut 1 H.

Assemble the ray portion of this block using the Foundation Piecing method (page 10). The foundation pattern is on page 77. Note that pieces A–G are cut oversize for the Foundation Piecing method.

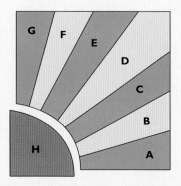

Assemble this block using the Flip and Sew method (page 17).

CUTTING

From Fabric 1:
Cut 3 squares $2\frac{1}{8}'' \times 2\frac{1}{8}''$; cut each square once diagonally to yield 2 half-square triangles (6 total) (A1). You will have 1 triangle left over.

Cut 2 rectangles $1\frac{3}{4}'' \times 3''$ (C).

Cut 2 rectangles $1\frac{5}{8}'' \times 4\frac{1}{4}''$ (D).

Cut 1 rectangle $1'' \times 6\frac{1}{2}''$ (F1).

From Fabric 2:
Cut 3 squares $2\frac{1}{8}'' \times 2\frac{1}{8}''$; cut each square once diagonally to yield 2 half-square triangles (6 total) (A2). You will have 1 triangle left over.

Cut 2 squares $1\frac{3}{4}'' \times 1\frac{3}{4}''$ (B2).

From Fabric 3:
Cut 1 rectangle $1\frac{3}{4}'' \times 6\frac{1}{2}''$ (E).

From Fabric 4:
Cut 2 squares $1\frac{3}{4}'' \times 1\frac{3}{4}''$ (B4).

Cut 1 rectangle $1'' \times 6\frac{1}{2}''$ (F4).

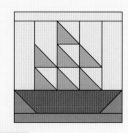

Make 2.

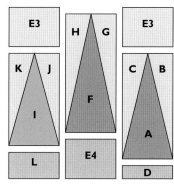

Assemble the treetop portions of this block using the Foundation Piecing method (page 10). The foundation patterns are on page 78. Note that pieces A–C and F–K are cut oversize for the Foundation Piecing method.

CUTTING

From Fabric 1:
Cut 2 rectangles $3'' \times 5\frac{1}{2}''$ (A and F).

From Fabric 2:
Cut 1 rectangle $3'' \times 4\frac{1}{2}''$ (I).

From Fabric 3:
Cut 4 rectangles $2'' \times 5\frac{1}{2}''$ (B, C, G, and H).

Cut 2 rectangles $2\frac{1}{2}'' \times 2''$ (E3).

Cut 2 rectangles $2'' \times 4\frac{1}{2}''$ (J and K).

From Fabric 4:
Cut 1 rectangle $1'' \times 2\frac{1}{2}''$ (D).

Cut 1 rectangle $2\frac{1}{2}'' \times 2''$ (E4).

Cut 1 rectangle $2\frac{1}{2}'' \times 1\frac{1}{2}''$ (L).

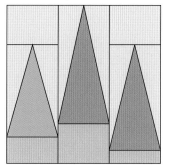

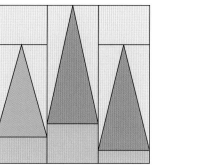

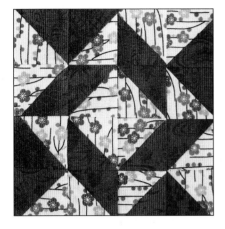

CUTTING

From *each* of Fabrics 1 and 2:

Cut 8 squares $2\frac{5}{8}'' \times 2\frac{5}{8}''$; cut each square once diagonally to yield 2 half-square triangles (16 from each fabric) (A1 and A2).

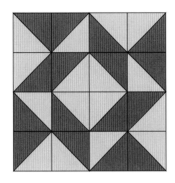

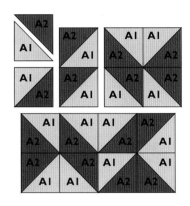

CUTTING

4" Block

From *each* of Fabrics 1 and 2:

Cut 1 square $3\frac{1}{4}'' \times 3\frac{1}{4}''$; cut twice diagonally to yield 4 quarter-square triangles (A1 and A2).

From Fabric 3:

Cut 2 squares $2\frac{7}{8}'' \times 2\frac{7}{8}''$; cut once diagonally to yield 2 half-square triangles (4 total) (B).

6" Block

From each of Fabrics 1 and 2:

Cut 1 square $4\frac{1}{4}'' \times 4\frac{1}{4}''$; cut twice diagonally to yield 4 quarter-square triangles (A1 and A2).

From Fabric 3:

Cut 2 squares $3\frac{7}{8}'' \times 3\frac{7}{8}''$; cut once diagonally to yield 2 half-square triangles (4 total) (B).

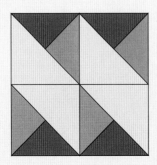

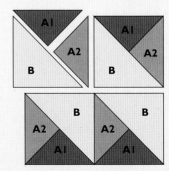

Beautiful Borders: PIECED AND PLAIN

The quilts in this book include a combination of pieced and plain (i.e., unpieced) borders, which is a typical combination for medallion quilts. This chapter includes three different borders to try, but you can come up with countless pieced-border variations by combining the blocks in the Block Gallery (pages 20–34). See Alternate Pieced Border Suggestions (page 41) for inspiration.

PICKET FENCE BORDER

Finished Size: 4″ × 35″

Yardages and instructions are for one border.

MATERIALS

All yardage is based on fabric that is 40″ wide after laundering.

⅓ yard Fabric 1 for the background

⅓ yard Fabric 2 for the fence

CUTTING

Cut strips across the fabric width (selvage to selvage).

From Fabric 1:

Cut 3 strips 1½″ × 40″.

Cut 9 squares 1⅞″ × 1⅞″; cut each square once diagonally to yield 2 half-square triangles (18 total). You will have 1 triangle left over.

From Fabric 2:

Cut 2 strips 1″ × 40″.

Cut 9 squares 1⅞″ × 1⅞″; cut each square once diagonally to yield 2 half-square triangles (18 total). You will have 1 triangle left over.

Cut 2 strips 1½″ × 40″; crosscut into 17 pieces, 1½″ × 3½″.

ASSEMBLING THE BORDER

1. Sew together the 1½″ × 40″ Fabric 1 strips and the 1″ × 40″ Fabric 2 strips, alternating them to make a strip set. Press. Cut 18 segments, each 1½″ wide.

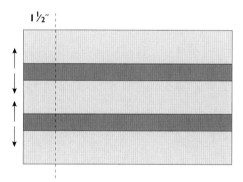

Cut 18 segments.

2. Sew together a Fabric 1 triangle and a Fabric 2 triangle to make a half-square triangle unit. Press. Make 17.

Make 17.

Make 17.

3. Sew a unit from Step 2 to each 1½″ × 3½″ Fabric 2 piece, taking care to position the triangle units as shown. Press. Make 17.

4. Arrange the segments from Step 1 and the units from Step 3, alternating them as shown. Press.

TWINKLE STAR BORDER

Finished Size: 6″ × 35″

Yardages and instructions are for one border.

MATERIALS

All yardage is based on fabric that is 40″ wide after laundering, unless noted otherwise.

½ yard Fabric 1 for background

¼ yard Fabric 2 for stars

CUTTING

Cut all strips across the fabric width (selvage to selvage). See tip at right for explanation of asterisked entries.

From Fabric 1:

Cut 4 strips 1½″ × 40″; crosscut into:

    33 squares 1½″ × 1½″.

    2 rectangles 1½″ × 2½″.

    16 rectangles 1½″ × 3½″.

    2 rectangles 1½″ × 6½″.*

Cut 2 strips 1⅞″ × 40″; crosscut into 32 squares 1⅞″ × 1⅞″. Cut each square once diagonally to yield 2 half-square triangles (64 total).

Cut 2 strips 1″ × 33½″.**

From Fabric 2:

Cut 1 strip 1½″ × 40″; crosscut into 16 squares 1½″ × 1½″.

Cut 2 strips 1⅞″ × 40″; crosscut into 32 squares 1⅞″ × 1⅞″. Cut each square once diagonally to yield 2 half-square triangles (64 total).

SIMPLE ALTERATIONS! You can easily adjust the length and/or width of this border to accommodate side and bottom borders and corner blocks made from 7″ blocks, such as Port and Starboard (page 30) or Ocean Wave (page 29). Simply cut the Fabric 1 side pieces (*) 1½″ × 7½″ and the Fabric 1 top and bottom strips (**) 1½″ × 33½″.

ASSEMBLING THE BORDER

1. Sew together a Fabric 1 triangle and a Fabric 2 triangle to make a half-square triangle unit. Press. Make 64.

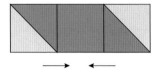

Make 64.

2. Arrange and sew 2 units from Step 1 and a Fabric 2 square. Press. Make 16.

Make 16.

3. Arrange and sew a Fabric 1 square, 8 units from Step 1, and eight 1½″ × 3½″ Fabric 1 pieces, taking care to position the triangle units as shown. Press. Label this Row 1.

Row 1

4. Arrange and sew 8 units from Step 2, 7 Fabric 1 squares, and a 1½″ × 2½″ Fabric 1 piece, taking care to position the triangle units as shown. Press. Label this Row 2.

Row 2

5. Arrange and sew 16 units from Step 1 and 17 Fabric 1 squares, taking care to position the triangle units as shown. Press. Label this Row 3.

Row 3

6. Arrange and sew 8 units from Step 2, 7 Fabric 1 squares, and a 1½″ × 2½″ Fabric 1 piece, taking care to position the triangle units as shown. Press. Label this Row 4.

Row 4

7. Arrange and sew a Fabric 1 square, 8 units from Step 1, and eight 1½″ × 3½″ Fabric 1 pieces, taking care to position the triangle units as shown. Press. Label this Row 5.

Row 5

8. Arrange and sew the rows from Steps 3–7. Press.

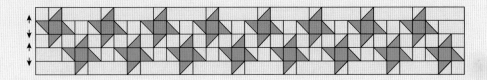

9. Sew a 1″ × 33½″ Fabric 1 piece to the top and bottom of the unit from Step 8. Press.

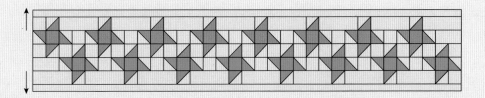

10. Sew a 1½″ × 6½″ Fabric 1 piece to the left and right edges of the unit from Step 9. Press.

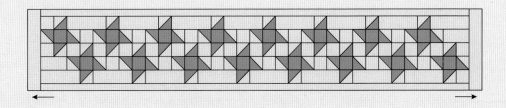

BARGELLO BORDER

Finished Size: *7″ × 49″*

Yardages and instructions are for two borders (top and bottom).

MATERIALS

This border can be made from fat quarters of fabric. A fat quarter measures 18″ × 21″.

1 fat quarter *each* of 12 different fabrics

CUTTING

Cut all strips across the width. Keep the strips sorted by fabric.

From *each* of Fabrics 1–12:
Cut 5 strips 1½″ × 20″.

From *each* of Fabrics 6–12:
Cut 1 square 1½″ × 1½″ (7 total).

ASSEMBLING THE BORDER

1. Arrange 1 of each strip (Fabrics 1–12) in a pleasing visual order. Sew the strips together to make a strip set. Make 3 identical strip sets. Press the seams in the same direction in each strip set.

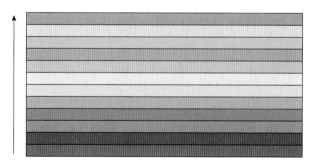

Make 3.

2. Cut a total of 32 segments, each 1½″ wide, from the strip sets you made in Step 1. Label these Segment 1.

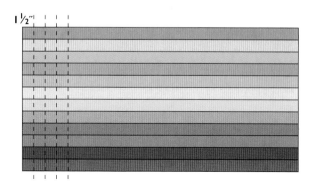

Segment 1; Cut 32.

3. Repeat Step 1, arranging the strips in the same order. Make 2 strip sets. Press the seams in the opposite direction than the Step 1 strip sets.

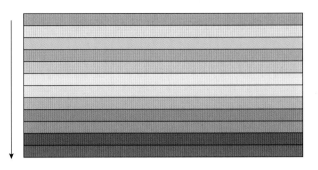

Make 2.

4. Cut a total of 24 segments, each 1½″ wide, from the strip sets you made in Step 3. Label these Segment 2.

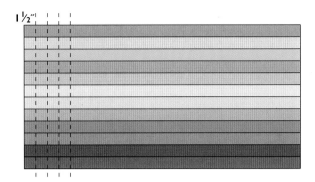

Segment 2; Cut 24.

5. Arrange and sew 4 Segment 1 units. Make 8. Press the seams in the same direction as the other seams, toward Fabric 1. Repeat using the Segment 2 units. Make 6. Press the seams in the same direction as the other seams, away from Fabric 1. Keep the newly stitched rows separated.

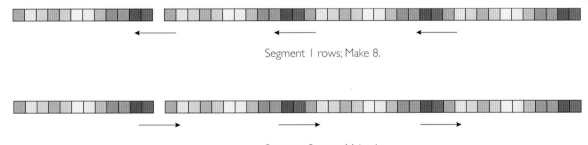

Segment 1 rows; Make 8.

Segment 2 rows; Make 6.

6. Starting with a Segment 1 row, arrange 7 rows, alternating Segment 1 and Segment 2 rows. Offset each row by one square along the left edge to create the Bargello effect.

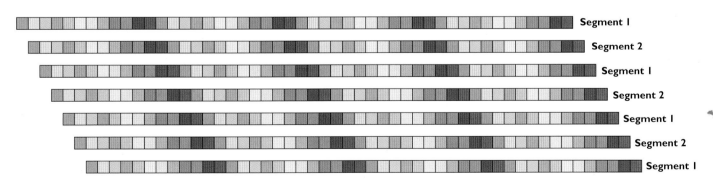

Segment 1
Segment 2
Segment 1
Segment 2
Segment 1
Segment 2
Segment 1

7. Undo the seams to remove the appropriate number of squares from the right edge of Rows 1–6.

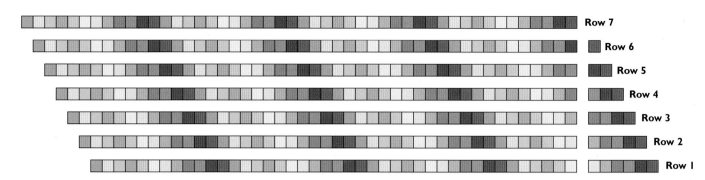

Row 7
Row 6
Row 5
Row 4
Row 3
Row 2
Row 1

8. Sew the squares removed in Step 7 to the left edge of the appropriate row.

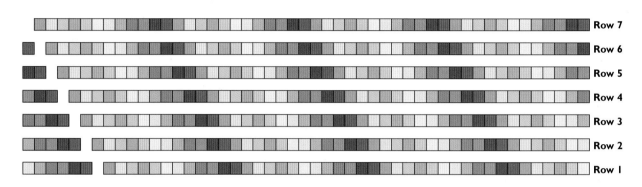

Row 7
Row 6
Row 5
Row 4
Row 3
Row 2
Row 1

9. Sew the appropriately colored 1½″ × 1½″ square to the left edge of each row (1–7).

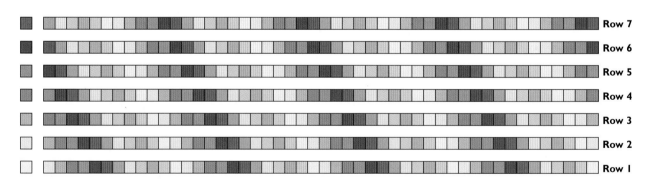

Row 7
Row 6
Row 5
Row 4
Row 3
Row 2
Row 1

10. Sew the rows together in order, carefully pinning the intersections to ensure an accurate match. Press.

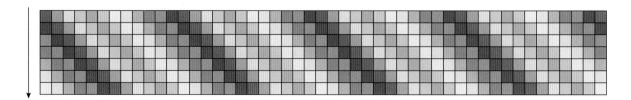

11. Repeat Steps 5–10 to make a second, identical border.

ALTERNATE PIECED BORDER SUGGESTIONS

You need only look through the wonderful collection of quilts scattered throughout this book to discover a wide variety of effective—and terrific—alternatives for pieced borders. The units and blocks in the Block Gallery (pages 20–34) are sized to allow you great flexibility and creativity in the combinations you select. They are also sized to fit together nicely with the presized borders in this chapter. Here are some ideas to get you started.

MATH CHALLENGED? Focus on selecting blocks and borders that are the same size; for example, combine blocks that finish 6″—such as Sailboat (page 31), Cry of the Loon (page 22), and Sawtooth Star (page 32)—with 6″-wide (finished) borders—such as Twinkle Star (page 36) and Picket Fence with extra top and bottom strips (page 35).

Choose a theme: If you flip through the Block Gallery, you'll notice that most of the blocks have a nautical or waterfront theme. If your Mariner's memories revolve around summers spent at a lakefront cabin, you might choose a combination of Sunrise (page 32), Coast Guard House (page 22), and a variety of tree blocks, such as Evergreen Tree and Filbert Tree (page 24), for a pieced border, as Susie Kincy did for her quilt *Land of Liberty* (page 62).

Border detail of
Land of Liberty

If your maritime adventures tend to be more of the deep-sea variety, you might prefer a mix of Fish (page 25) and Wild Waves (page 34), as in the bottom-border combination of Susie's quilt.

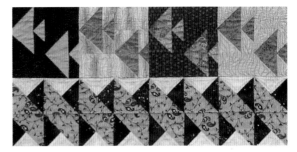

Border detail of *Land of Liberty*

Utilize theme fabrics: You've seen them out there, and we've discussed them already in Fabric (page 7): those fabulous nautical and landscape prints. While they are excellent choices for unpieced borders (see *I'd Rather Be Sailing*, by Marie L. Miller, on page 52), they can sometimes be cut into blocks for use in pieced borders. Keep an eye out for preprinted panels, too.

Border detail of *I'd Rather Be Sailing*

Make adaptations: This is your quilt! Don't be afraid to adapt any border—even the predesigned ones in this chapter—to suit your needs. John and Louise James did just that, turning Picket Fence (page 35) into a pier in *Northwest Compass* (page 63).

Border detail of *Northwest Compass*

Play with the individual border blocks, too. Turn the Coast Guard House (page 22) into a cottage by adding a path and some artful appliqués. Or try one of my favorite variations: substitute theme-related embroidery for a plain or printed fabric in any border block that features a large unpieced area, such as the Attic Window in *Voices From My Garden* (page 53).

These are just a few suggestions for designing unique borders for your Mariner's Medallion quilt. I'm sure you'll come up with many others. Enjoy the voyage!

Border detail of *Voices From My Garden*

THE GARDEN COURT COMPASS

63″ × 78″, designed, pieced, and quilted by M'Liss Rae Hawley, 1997. This quilt includes all three borders (Picket Fence, Twinkle Star, and Bargello) described in this chapter.

SQUARED BORDERS

Medallion quilts, with their multiple borders, have the potential to become busy—if not overwhelming! That's where plain—or cut-from-a-single-fabric—borders come to the rescue. They give the viewer's eye a place to rest amid all the pieced action. They also give you, the quiltmaker, a bit of creative *and* fudge room: you can easily adjust the border width to accommodate a pieced border that finishes a bit too short or too long or complement a border made from blocks in a size different from the project quilts.

The plain borders on the project quilts in this book feature squared corners; these are the easiest of all borders to sew. If necessary, piece strips together with straight seams to achieve the required length. Add the top and bottom borders first and then the side borders.

1. Measure the quilt top through the center from side to side and cut 2 border strips to this measurement. These will be the top and bottom borders.

2. Place pins at the center point of the top and bottom of the quilt top, as well as at the center point of each border strip. Pin the borders to the quilt top, matching the ends and center points. Use additional pins as needed, easing or gently stretching the border to fit.

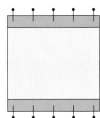

3. Sew the borders to the quilt with a ¼″ seam. Press as instructed—usually toward the border. If the quilt top is slightly longer than the border, stitch with the quilt top on the bottom, closest to the feed dogs. If the reverse is true, stitch with the border on the bottom. The motion of the feed dogs will help ease in the extra length.

4. Measure the quilt top from top to bottom, including the borders you've just sewn, and cut 2 border strips to this measurement. These will be the side borders. Repeat Steps 2 and 3 to pin, sew, and press the borders.

Queen Isabel's Pillow, 18″ × 18″ made by Marie L. Miller, 2005.

43

THE MARINER'S MEDALLION
WALLHANGING

Viva Las Vegas, designed and pieced by M'Liss Rae Hawley, 2005. Machine quilted by Barbara Dau.

he Mariner's Medallion Wallhanging is the perfect size quilt for your home or office and makes a wonderful first-time foundation-piecing project. The compass goes together quickly and is finished with a simple, traditionally pieced border of Flying Geese, a narrow accent border, and a wider outer border.

Why not make this little quilt to commemorate an event, trip, holiday, season, or favorite fabric? My quilt *Viva Las Vegas* is reminiscent of business and pleasure trips to Las Vegas.

MATERIALS

All yardage is based on fabric that is 40″ wide after laundering. Materials (and cut sizes) for the 16½″ Mariner's Compass appear under the cutting instructions for Making the Mariner's Compass Block (page 10).

⅔ yard for the Mariner's Compass block background square

½ yard *each* of 2 contrasting fabrics for the Flying Geese border (Fabric 1 and Fabric 2)

¼ yard for the accent border

⅔ yard for the outer border

½ yard for the binding

2⅝ yards for the backing

46″ × 46″ piece of batting

CUTTING

Cut all strips across the fabric width.

From the Flying Geese Fabric 1:
Cut 6 strips 2½″ × 40″; crosscut into 96 squares 2½″ × 2½″.

From the Flying Geese Fabric 2:
Cut 6 strips 2½″ × 40″; crosscut into 48 rectangles 2½″ × 4½″.

From the background square fabric:
Cut 1 square 20½″ × 20½″.

From the accent border fabric:
Cut 4 strips 1″ × 40″.

From the outer border fabric:
Cut 4 strips 5″ × 40″.

From the binding fabric:
Cut 5 strips 3″ × 40″.

MARINER'S COMPASS BLOCK

1. Refer to Making the Mariner's Compass Block (page 10) and the patterns on pages 73–74. Use Fabrics A–E to construct a 16½″-diameter Mariner's Compass circle.

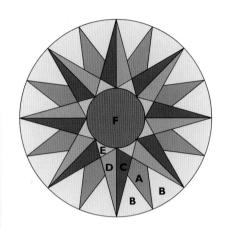

2. Use your preferred appliqué method to stitch the unit from Step 1 to the 20½″ Mariner's Compass block background square. Appliqué the center circle to the compass.

QUILT ASSEMBLY

1. Refer to the Flip and Sew method (page 17) and the Flying Geese instructions (page 25). Use the 2½″ × 2½″ Fabric 1 squares and the 2½″ × 4½″ Fabric 2 rectangles to construct 48 Flying Geese units. Press.

Make 48.

2. Sew together 10 Flying Geese units from Step 1 to make a row. Press. Make 4. Sew a row to the top and bottom of the quilt. Press.

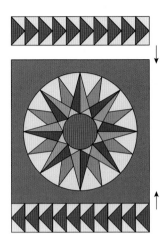

3. Sew together the remaining Flying Geese units from Step 1 in pairs. Press. Make 4. Sew 2 units to opposite ends of each remaining row from Step 2. Press. Make 2. Sew to the sides of the quilt. Press.

Make 4.

4. Refer to Squared Borders (page 43). Measure, trim, and sew a 1″-wide accent border strip to the top and bottom of the quilt. Press the seams toward this border. Repeat to sew 1″-wide accent borders to the sides. Press.

5. Measure, trim, and sew a 5″-wide outer border strip to the top and bottom of the quilt. Press the seams toward this outer border. Repeat to sew 5″-wide outer borders to the sides. Press.

FINISHING

Refer to Finishing Your Quilt (page 70).

1. Piece and press the backing.

2. Layer the quilt top, batting, and backing; baste.

3. Hand or machine quilt as desired.

4. Use the 3″-wide strips to bind the edges of the quilt.

5. Add a hanging sleeve and label if desired.

KOI IN MARINER'S GARDEN
41½″ × 41½″, pieced by Anastasia Riordan, 2005. Machine quilted by Barbara Dau.

MARINER'S COMPASS WITH RED KOI
38″ × 38″, pieced by Annette Barca, 2005. Machine quilted by Barbara Dau.

THE MARINER'S FAVORITE STOWAWAY

39½" × 39½", pieced by Carla Zimmermann, 2005.
Machine quilted by Kim McKinnon.

**ORIENTAL LEGENDS WHISPER
BENEATH THE WAVES**

44" × 44", pieced by Carla Zimmermann,
2005. Machine quilted by Barbara Dau.

THE MARINER'S MEDALLION
LAP QUILT

Dream Guide, designed and pieced by M'Liss Rae Hawley, 2005. Machine quilted by Barbara Dau.

he Mariner's Medallion Lap Quilt features a 16½″ compass appliquéd to a 19″ × 19″ (finished) square and surrounded by a series of pieced and plain borders. For *Dream Guide*, I selected fabrics from my Kimono Art fabric line . My version expresses an Asian influence with bright colors and embroideries from the coordinating Kimono Art embroidery collection (see Resources on page 72).

FINISHED QUILT SIZE: 49″ × 58″

Schematic

MATERIALS

All yardage is based on fabric that is 40″ wide after laundering.

⅔ yard for the Mariner's Compass block background square

¼ yard for the first accent border

¼ yard for the second accent border

⅜ yard for the third accent border

1¼ yards for the outer border

⅝ yard for the binding

3⅞ yards for the backing

57″ × 66″ piece of batting

CUTTING

Cut all strips across the fabric width.

From the background square fabric:
Cut 1 square 19½″ × 19½″.

From the first accent border fabric:
Cut 2 strips 1½″ × 19½″.

Cut 2 strips 1½″ × 21½″.

From the second accent border fabric:
Cut 2 strips 1½″ × 35½″.

Cut 2 strips 1″ × 37½″.

From the third accent border fabric:
Cut 5 strips 1½″ × 40″.

From the outer border fabric:
Cut 6 strips 6″ × 40″.

From the binding fabric:
Cut 6 strips 3″ × 40″.

Materials and cutting specifications listed are for the Mariner's Compass background block, borders, backing, and binding. Materials (and cut sizes) for the 16½″ Mariner's Compass are listed under the cutting instructions for Making the Mariner's Compass Block (page 10). Materials for individual border blocks will depend on the selection made and can be found in the Block Gallery (pages 20–34). The quilt shown uses a combination of three 7″ (finished) blocks for the first pieced border: four Port and Starboard blocks (page 30), eight 7″ Arctic Nights blocks (page 20), and four Mariner's Embroidery blocks (page 29). The second pieced border uses eighteen 4″ Wild Waves blocks (page 34). If you wish, you can substitute any combination of 7″ and 4″ blocks (or units) for these borders, mixing and matching as you please. Refer to the schematic as needed.

MARINER'S COMPASS BLOCK

1. Refer to Making the Mariner's Compass Block (page 10) and the patterns on pages 73–74. Use Fabrics A–E to construct a 16½"-diameter Mariner's Compass circle.

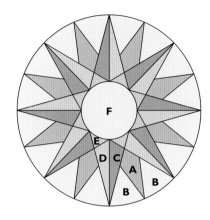

2. Use your preferred appliqué method to stitch the unit from Step 1 to the 19½" Mariner's Compass block background square. Appliqué the center circle to the compass.

QUILT ASSEMBLY

1. Refer to Squared Borders (page 43), the quilt photo (page 48), and the assembly diagram (at far right). Sew the 1½" × 19½" first accent border strips to the top and bottom of the Mariner's Compass block. Press the seams toward the border. Sew the 1½" × 20½" first accent border strips to the sides. Press.

2. Make and sew together three 7" blocks to make a border row. (I used 2 Arctic Night blocks and 1 Port and Starboard block.) Make 4 rows. Refer to the quilt photo and assembly diagram. Sew a row to the top and bottom of the quilt. Press the seams toward the accent border.

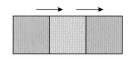

Make 4.

3. Make and sew 4 additional 7" blocks. (I used the Mariner's Embroidery block.) Sew a block to opposite ends of each remaining row from Step 2. Press. Make 2. Sew to the sides of the quilt. Press.

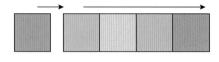

Make 2.

4. Sew the 1½" × 35½" second accent border strips to the top and bottom of the quilt. Press the seams toward the border. Sew the 1" × 37½" second accent border strips to the sides. Press.

5. Make and sew together nine 4" blocks to make a border row. (I used the Wild Waves block.) Make 2 rows. Refer to the quilt photo and assembly diagram. Sew a row to the top and bottom of the quilt. Press the seams toward the accent border.

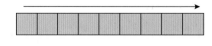

Make 2.

6. Measure, trim, and sew a 1½"-wide third accent border strip to the top and bottom of the quilt. Press the seams toward this border. Repeat to sew 1½"-wide third accent borders to the sides, piecing as necessary. Press.

7. Repeat Step 6 to measure, trim, and sew 6"-wide outer border strips to the top, bottom, and sides of the quilt. Press.

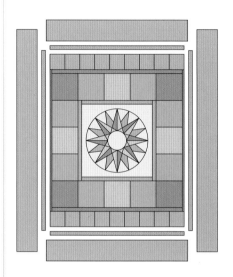

Assembly diagram

FINISHING

Refer to Finishing Your Quilt (page 70).

1. Piece and press the backing.

2. Layer the quilt top, batting, and backing; baste.

3. Hand or machine quilt as desired.

4. Use the 3"-wide strips to bind the edges of the quilt.

5. Add a hanging sleeve and label if desired.

MY BEAUTIFUL BALLOON
44″ × 44″, pieced by Susie Kincy, 2005.
Machine quilted by Barbara Dau.

SUMMER SUNSETS
46½″ × 55½″, pieced by Vicki
DeGraaf, 2005. Machine quilted
by Barbara Dau.

FROM CHAOS TO ORDER
51″ × 66″, pieced by Marie L. Miller, 2005.
Machine quilted by Barbara Dau.

I'D RATHER BE SAILING
55½″ × 63½″, pieced by Marie L. Miller, 2005.
Machine quilted by Barbara Dau.

THE MARINER'S MEDALLION ON POINT

Voices From My Garden, designed and pieced by M'Liss Rae Hawley, 2005. Machine quilted by Barbara Dau.

This version of the Mariner's Medallion is a smaller-size compass set on point. The 6″ blocks surrounding the compass lend themselves to many different themes. My quilt *Voices From My Garden* is a celebration of our pets and garden. The Attic Window blocks feature embroideries from a variety of my embroidery collections and represent our yard throughout the year. See the tip box on page 55 and Resources on page 72 for additional information.

Schematic

Materials and cutting specifications listed are for the Mariner's Compass background block, borders, backing, and binding. Materials (and cut sizes) for the 11″ Mariner's Compass are listed under the cutting instructions for Making the Mariner's Compass Block (page 11). Materials for individual border blocks will depend on the selection made and can be found in the Block Gallery (pages 20–34). The quilt shown uses a combination of three different 6″ (finished) blocks for the first pieced border: ten Sawtooth Star blocks (page 32), nine Attic Window blocks (page 20), and one foundation-pieced Sunrise block (page 32). The second pieced border uses twenty Flying Geese blocks (page 25) for the top border and a variation of the Picket Fence border (page 35) for the bottom border. If you wish, you can substitute any combination of 6″ and 4″ blocks or border units for these borders, mixing and matching as you please. Refer to the schematic as needed.

MATERIALS

All yardage is based on fabric that is 40″ wide after laundering.

½ yard for the Mariner's Compass block background square

½ yard for the center setting triangles

¼ yard for the first accent border

⅓ yard for the second accent border

½ yard for the third accent border

⅓ yard for the fourth accent border

1¼ yards for the outer border

⅔ yard for the binding

4 yards for the backing

61″ × 69″ piece of batting

CUTTING

Cut all strips across the fabric width.

From the background square fabric:
Cut 1 square 12½″ × 12½″.

From the center setting triangle fabric:
Cut 2 squares 12″ × 12″; cut each square once diagonally to yield 2 half-square triangles (2 total).

From the first accent border fabric:
Cut 2 strips 1½″ × 12½″.

Cut 2 strips 1½″ × 14½″.

From the second accent border fabric:
Cut 2 strips 2″ × 21½″.

Cut 2 strips 2″ × 24½″.

From the third accent border fabric:
Cut 5 strips 2½″ × 40″.

From the fourth accent border fabric:
Cut 5 strips 1½″ × 40″.

From the outer border fabric:
Cut 6 strips 6″ × 40″.

From the binding fabric:
Cut 7 strips 3″ × 40″.

MARINER'S COMPASS BLOCK

1. Refer to Making the Mariner's Compass Block (page 10) and the patterns on pages 73–74. Use Fabrics A–E to construct an 11″-diameter Mariner's Compass circle.

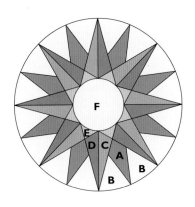

2. Use your preferred appliqué method to stitch the unit from Step 1 to the 12½″ Mariner's Compass block background square. Appliqué the center circle to the compass.

QUILT ASSEMBLY

1. Refer to Squared Borders (page 43), the quilt photo (page 53), and the assembly diagram (page 56). Sew the 1½″ × 12½″ first accent border strips to the top and bottom of the block. Press the seams toward the border. Sew the 1½″ × 14½″ first accent border strips to the sides. Press.

2. Center and sew a 12″ half-square triangle to opposite sides of the Mariner's Compass block. Press. Center

and sew half-square triangles to the remaining sides. The half-square triangles are slightly oversized to allow the Mariner's Compass block to float in the triangle area. Press.

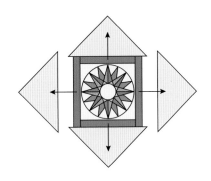

3. Sew the 2″ × 21½″ second accent border strips to the top and bottom of the unit from Step 1. Press the seams toward the border. Sew the 2″ × 24½″ first accent border strips to the sides. Press.

4. Make and sew four 6″ blocks together to make a border row. (I used 2 Sawtooth Star and 2 Attic Window blocks.) Make 4 rows, 2 of each variation. Sew a row to the top and bottom of the quilt. Press.

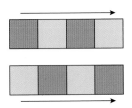

Make 2 of each variation.

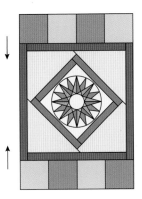

EYE-CATCHING EMBROIDERY! Decorative stitchery is a simple way to add colorful eye appeal to your Attic Window blocks. Refer to the instructions for the Attic Window block (page 20) but cut the Fabric 3 square slightly over sized (i.e., 7″ × 7″). When the embroidery is complete, trim the square to the correct measurement (5″ × 5″) and proceed to assemble the block.

5. Sew a 6″ block to opposite ends of each remaining row from Step 4. (I used a Sunrise and a Sawtooth Star block for one row and an Attic Window and a Sawtooth Star block for the other.) Press. Sew to the sides of the quilt. Press.

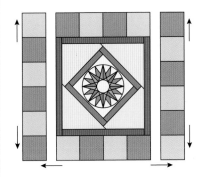

6. Measure, trim, and sew a 2½″-wide third accent border strip to the top and bottom of the quilt. Press the seams toward this border. Repeat to sew 2½″-wide third accent borders to the sides, piecing as necessary. Press.

7. Refer to the Flip and Sew method (page 17) and the Flying Geese instructions (page 25). Use the 2½″ × 2½″ Fabric 1 squares and the 2½″ × 4½″ Fabric 2 rectangles to construct 20 Flying Geese units. Press.

Make 20.

8. Sew together the Flying Geese units from Step 7 to make a row. Press. Refer to the quilt photo and assembly diagram. Sew the row to the top of the quilt. Press the seams toward the accent border.

9. Refer to Picket Fence Border (page 35). Make a Picket Fence border using the modifications described in the box below. Refer to the quilt photo and assembly diagram. Sew the border to the bottom of the quilt. Press the seams toward the accent border.

10. Measure, trim, and sew a 1½″-wide fourth accent border strip to the top and bottom of the quilt, piecing as necessary. Press the seams toward this border. Repeat to sew 1½″-wide fourth accent borders to the sides, piecing as necessary. Press.

11. Repeat Step 6 to measure, trim, and sew 6″-wide outer border strips to the top, bottom, and sides of the quilt. Press.

FINISHING

Refer to Finishing Your Quilt (page 70).

1. Piece and press the backing.

2. Layer the quilt top, batting, and backing; baste.

3. Hand or machine quilt as desired.

4. Use the 3″-wide strips to bind the edges of the quilt.

5. Add a hanging sleeve and label if desired.

Assembly diagram

I needed to make the Picket Fence border slightly longer to fit this quilt. Here's the method I used:

1. Cut the pieces described in the cutting instructions for Picket Fence Border (page 35). Cut an additional 1⅞″ × 1⅞″ square from Fabric 1 and an additional 1⅞″ × 1⅞″ square and 1½″ × 3½″ piece from Fabric 2. Cut each square once diagonally to make 2 half-square triangles (4 total).

2. Cut the eighteen 1½″-wide segments described in Assembling the Border, Step 1 (page 35). Cut 2 additional 2″-wide segments.

3. Use the 1⅞″ Fabric 1 and Fabric 2 squares to make half-square triangle units, as described in Assembling the Border, Step 2 (page 35). You will have 19 units total.

4. Sew each unit from Step 3 to a 1½″ × 3½″ Fabric 2 piece. You will have 19 units total.

5. Arrange the units and segments from Steps 2 and 4 as shown. Press. The new border measures 4½″ high × 40½″ wide (unfinished).

That's all there is to it! You can adjust the length of this border as you wish by making simple alterations such as these.

BYGONE DAYS

55″ × 63″, pieced by Susie Kincy, 2005. Machine quilted by Barbara Dau.

FLOWERS IN BLOOM
53″ × 61″, pieced by Suzanne Neil, 2005.
Machine quilted by Stacie Johnson and
Debbie Webster.

VINTAGE AMERICANA
53½″ × 62″, pieced by Barbara Higbee-Price,
2005. Machine quilted by Barbara Dau.

THE MARINER'S MEDALLION
FULL-SIZE QUILT

My Canvas to the World, designed and pieced by M Liss Rae Hawley, 2006. Machine quilted by Barbara Dau.

hen I designed the original Mariner's Medallion quilt, *The Garden Court Compass* (page 42), I planned it for a block-of-the-month class. I wanted to incorporate as many piecing techniques as possible. The quilt represents our home on Whidbey Island from the lighthouse and Coast Guard house to the filbert and evergreen trees.

My Canvas to the World continues my adventure with the Mariner's Medallion. I used more than 50 brightly hued batik fabrics in this happy quilt, reflecting my love of exuberant color.

Schematic

Materials and cutting specifications listed are for the Mariner's Compass background block, borders, backing, and binding. Materials (and cut sizes) for the 16½″ Mariner's Compass are listed under the cutting instructions for Making the Mariner's Compass Block (page 10). I used one Twinkle Star border (page 36), one Picket Fence border (page 35), and top and bottom Bargello borders (page 38). I created unique side borders by selecting blocks from the Block Gallery (pages 20–34). For the left pieced border, starting from the top, I used one 6″ foundation-pieced Sunrise block (page 32), one 6″ × 5″ Lodgepole Pines block (page 28), one 6″ × 6¼″ Filbert Tree block (page 24), one 6″ Chinese Junk block (page 21), one 6″ Evergreen Tree block (page 24), one 6″ × 3½″ embroidered filler strip, and one 6″ × 12¼″ Lighthouse block (page 27). For the right pieced border, starting from the top, I used one 6″ Ohio Star block (page 30), one 6″ Evergreen Tree block (page 24), one 6″ × 6″ embroidered filler strip, one 6″ × 6¼″ Filbert Tree block (page 24), one 6″ Sailboat block (page 31), one 6″ × 5″ Lodgepole Pines block (page 28), and one 6″ × 9¼″ Coast Guard House block (page 22). If you wish, you can substitute any combination of blocks, units, or filler strips for these borders, mixing and matching as you please, so long as they total the measurement indicated in the instructions. Refer to the schematic as needed.

MATERIALS

All yardage is based on fabric that is 40″ wide after laundering.

⅔ yard for the Mariner's Compass block background square

¼ yard for the first accent border

½ yard for the second accent border

⅙ yard for the top frame

¼ yard for the bottom frame 1

⅙ yard for the bottom frame 2

⅓ yard for the third accent border

⅓ yard for the fourth accent border

1⅔ yards for the outer border

⅞ yard for the binding

5 yards for the backing

73″ × 88″ piece of batting

CUTTING

Cut all strips across the fabric width.

From the background square fabric:
Cut 1 square 20½″ × 20½″.

From the first accent border fabric:
Cut 2 strips 1½″ × 28½″.

Cut 2 strips 1½″ × 30½″.

From the second accent border fabric:
Cut 2 strips 3″ × 30½″.

Cut 2 strips 3″ × 35½″.

From the top frame fabric:
Cut 2 strips 1½″ × 40″.

From the bottom frame fabric 1:
Cut 2 strips 2″ × 40″.

From the bottom frame fabric 2:
Cut 2 strips 1½″ × 40″.

From the third accent border fabric:
Cut 6 strips 1½″ × 40″.

From the fourth accent border fabric:
Cut 6 strips 1½″ × 40″.

From the outer border fabric:
Cut 7 strips 7½″ × 40″.

From the binding fabric:
Cut 8 strips 3″ × 40″.

MARINER'S COMPASS BLOCK

1. Refer to Making the Mariner's Compass Block (page 10) and the patterns on pages 73–74. Use Fabrics A–E to construct a 16½″-diameter Mariner's Compass circle.

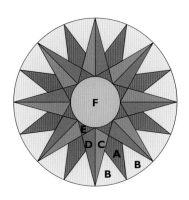

2. Use your preferred appliqué method to stitch the unit from Step 1 to the 20½″ Mariner's Compass block background square. Appliqué the center circle to the compass.

QUILT ASSEMBLY

1. Refer to the Flip and Sew method (page 17) and the Flying Geese instructions (page 25). Use the 2½″ × 2½″ Fabric 1 squares and the 2½″ × 4½″ Fabric 2 rectangles to construct 48 Flying Geese units. Press.

Make 48.

2. Sew together 10 Flying Geese units from Step 1 to make a row. Press. Make 4. Sew a row to the top and bottom of the quilt. Press.

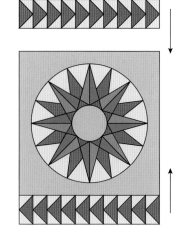

3. Sew together the remaining Flying Geese units from Step 1 in pairs. Press. Make 4. Sew 2 units to opposite ends of each remaining row from Step 2. Press. Make 2. Sew to the sides of the quilt. Press.

Make 4.

4. Refer to Squared Borders (page 43), the quilt photo (page 59), and the assembly diagram (page 62). Sew a 1½″ × 28½″ first accent border strip to the top and bottom of the quilt. Press the seams toward this border. Repeat to sew 1½″ × 30½″ first accent borders to the sides. Press.

5. Sew the 3″ × 30½″ second accent border strips to the top and bottom of the quilt. Press the seams toward this border. Sew the 3″ × 35½″ second accent border strips to the sides. Press.

6. Refer to Twinkle Star Border (page 36), the quilt photo, and the assembly diagram. Make a Twinkle Star border and sew it to the top of the quilt. Press the seams toward the accent border.

7. Refer to Picket Fence Border (page 35), the quilt photo, and the assembly diagram. Make a Picket Fence border and sew it to the bottom of the quilt. Press the seams toward the accent border.

8. Make and sew together blocks to make a left side border row that measures 6½″ wide × 45½″ long (unfinished). (See my choices in the box on page 60.) Refer to the quilt photo and assembly diagram and sew the row to the left side of the quilt. Press the seams toward the accent border.

9. Make and sew together blocks to make a right side border row that measures 6½″ wide × 45½″ long (unfinished). (See my choices in the box on page 60.) Refer to the quilt photo and assembly diagram and sew the row to the right side of the quilt. Press the seams toward the accent border.

10. Measure, trim, and sew a 1½″-wide top frame strip to the top and a 2″-wide bottom frame 1 strip to the bottom of the quilt, piecing as necessary. Press the seams toward the strips. Sew a 1½″-wide bottom frame 2 strip to the bottom of the quilt. Press.

11. Measure, trim, and sew a 1½″-wide third accent border strip to the top and bottom of the quilt, piecing as necessary. Press the seams toward this border. Repeat to sew 1½″-wide third accent borders to the sides. Press.

12. Refer to Bargello Border (page 38), the quilt photo, and the assembly diagram. Make 2 Bargello borders and sew to the top and bottom of the quilt. (For this quilt, I offset the right edge of the border rather than the left to create a mirror image of the border on page 40.) Press the seams toward the accent border.

13. Repeat Step 12 to measure, trim, and sew 1½″-wide fourth accent border strips and 7½″-wide outer border strips to the top, bottom, and sides of the quilt. Press.

FINISHING

Refer to Finishing Your Quilt (page 70).

1. Piece and press the backing.

2. Layer the quilt top, batting, and backing; baste.

3. Hand or machine quilt as desired.

4. Use the 3″-wide strips to bind the edges of the quilt.

5. Add a hanging sleeve and label if desired.

Assembly diagram

LAND OF LIBERTY

66½″ × 78″, pieced by Susie Kincy, 2005. Machine quilted by Barbara Dau.

LOOK WHAT M'LISS STARTED

51″ × 66″, pieced by Susie Kincy, 2005.
Machine quilted by Barbara Dau.

OUR GARDEN IN AUTUMN

66″ × 81″, pieced by Annette Barca,
2005. Machine quilted by Kim McKinnon.

LOOKING WEST

50″ × 50″, pieced and quilted
by Vicki DeGraaf, 1998.

NORTHWEST COMPASS

51″ × 66″, pieced by John and Louise James, 2005.
Machine quilted by Kim McKinnon.

Embellishing Your
MARINER'S MEDALLION QUILT

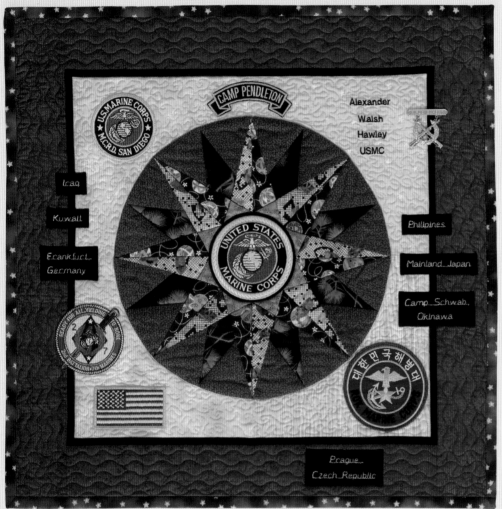

TOUR OF DUTY,
22½″ × 22½″, designed and pieced by
M'Liss Rae Hawley, started in 2001.
Tour of Duty is a work in progress,
made to document and honor our
son Alexander's service in the U.S.
Marine Corps. The compass is placed
on a background of four squares of
yellow fabric. The binding, a star print
from one of my fabric collections,
continues the theme. I incorporated
embroidered patches from some of
the places he has been stationed
and appliquéd machine-embroidered
labels from other locations as well.

I guess it's no secret that I *love* embellishment and what it can do to enhance a quilt surface. Happily, Mariner's Medallion quilts offer many opportunities for embellishment—enhancing with decorative threads and stitchery, as well as with beads, buttons, and unique appliqués. You can use any number of techniques to attach embellishments to your quilt. You can stitch, tie, glue, bead, or button them on or secure them with patches of see-through organza or vinyl. Your only limit is your imagination.

Embellishment can play many roles in your quilt's design. You can use these design elements to do the following:

- Add drama.
- Introduce whimsy.
- Emphasize the theme.
- Focus attention on a particular area of the quilt.
- Create filler strips or blocks to balance the quilt's setting.
- Even cover up mistakes!

In the following pages are some ideas for embellishing your Mariner's Medallion quilt.

MACHINE EMBROIDERY

Machine embroidery is one of my favorite techniques for embellishment. If you've never tried it before, a Mariner's Medallion quilt is the perfect canvas to give it a try.

You can incorporate machine embroidery into pieced blocks in place of a plain fabric square, as I did in the Attic Window blocks of *Voices From My Garden* (page 53).

You can use it to create unique filler strips, such as the ones I incorporated into the rows of *My Canvas to the World* (page 59).

You can use it to bring additional focus and detail to the center circle of the compass while reinforcing the theme of the quilt, as demonstrated by Anastasia Riordan in *Koi in Mariner's Garden* (page 46).

However you choose to introduce machine embroidery into your work, here are some tips to help you get started:

- Prewash the fabric you plan to use as the background for the embroidery designs.

- Begin with a fresh, new needle and change it during the process if the point becomes dull. Some embroidery designs have in excess of 10,000 stitches. A dull needle can distort the design.

- Outfit your machine with an embroidery-foot attachment.

- Prewind several bobbins with polyester or cotton bobbin-fill thread, such as Robison-Anton polyfilament bobbin thread, or purchase prewound bobbins, such as those manufactured by Robison-Anton. Bobbin

Use an embroidery foot to create beautiful machine embroidery.

thread in white or black or to match the background fabric are all good choices. Or you might prefer to change the bobbin thread as the color of the top thread changes, especially if the embroidery is an appliqué you'll see from both sides.

- Select a fabric stabilizer to use under the fabric. There are many different types of stabilizers available; whichever you choose, read the manufacturer's instructions *carefully*. When machine embroidering on 100% cotton fabric, I prefer a tear-away stabilizer, such as Inspira Tear-Away Stabilizer or Sulky of America's Tear Easy (medium weight). Sometimes a liquid stabilizer works well with a lightweight or light-colored fabric. If the fabric is prone to puckering, try a water- or heat-soluble stabilizer.

- A hoop keeps the fabric from shifting as you embroider the designs. If possible, place the fabric in the hoop so it is on the straight of grain, pleat- and pucker-free, and taut but not pulled too tight.

  If the block or the quilt section you are working on is too small for the hoop, stitch a piece of waste fabric to the edges. Remove this piece when you have completed the embroidery.

- Stitch a test of the desired embroidery, design using the fabric, threads, and stabilizer you plan to use for the project. You will be able to tell whether the thread tension is correct, whether the thread coverage is sufficient, and how the embroidered design will look on the background fabric you've chosen. You can then make any necessary adjustments. If you wish, you can incorporate your test design into your label or quilt backing.

APPLIQUÉS

Whether you create them yourself from fabric or embroidery or take advantage of the many terrific prepared motifs available at your quilt shop or sewing store, appliqués can

add personal meaning, a touch of playfulness, or an unexpected but welcome visual surprise to your Mariner's Medallion quilt.

For example, I used a variety of meaningful pre-embroidered patches to *Tour of Duty*, shown in detail above.

In *Looking West* (page 63), Vicki DeGraaf added charming detail to the Coast Guard House border block by applying flower, dog, birdhouse, and other motifs cut from fabric. Note also the chain-stitched smoke coming from the chimney!

COUCHING

In couching, decorative threads or trims are layered over the quilt surface and stitched in place using a zigzag, serpentine, or other decorative stitch and the appropriate foot attachment on your sewing machine. You can couch with thread that matches the color of the trim or use a different color or texture (e.g., metallic thread) for contrast.

Think ribbons, yarns, threads, tassels, strips of fabric (flat, twisted, or braided), cording, rickrack, lace, and other decorative trims. All are wonderful candidates for couching. For example, Vicki DeGraaf couched dazzling decorative trim on the Lighthouse block

of *Looking West*. (She also added a touch of hand embroidery to suggest rays of light cast by the lighthouse beam.) I used couching in my quilt *The Garden Court Compass* (page 42) as well.

BEADS, BUTTONS, AND OTHER TRINKETS

Where to begin? Besides the "usual" buttons and beads, you can add just about any small three-dimensional goody to your quilt. Sequins, buckles, charms, tiny seashells, washers, "gems and jewels" from costume jewelry—all are fair game

in the hands of an inventive embellisher! Take a close look at the Coast Guard House block in my quilt *The Garden Court Compass*. See how a tiny button becomes a doorknob? You might also see some of our more "sociable" family members peeking from the windows!

I used a button for the doorknob on my Lighthouse block as well, adding a bit of machine embroidery to represent railing near the lighthouse roof.

Vicki DeGraaf used bugle beads to represent the latches on the lighthouse gate she pieced into the Picket Fence border of *Looking West*.

In the end, embellishment is all about detail. Pay attention. Take time to observe the direction your quilt is going. This is also an opportunity to take risks: use threads and other products that are new to you, attempt new techniques, and combine colors and textures in innovative ways. Most important, be creative and have fun with embellishment!

From Quilt Top
TO FINISHED QUILT

PREPARING YOUR QUILT FOR QUILTING

As with every step of quiltmaking, this step is important. Don't skimp here! Take time to layer properly and baste sufficiently. The results—a nice, flat quilt, free of puckers and bumps—will make you proud.

Batting and Backing

Since I prefer machine quilting, I usually use cotton batting in a heavier weight for bed quilts and wallhangings and in a lighter weight for clothing. You'll probably want to stick with lightweight batting for hand quilting. Polyester batting is a good choice for tied quilts.

No matter which type of batting you choose, cut the batting approximately 4″ larger than the quilt top on all sides.

You'll also want the quilt backing to be approximately 4″ larger than the quilt top on all sides. You'll sometimes need to piece the fabric to have a large enough backing piece. Prewash the backing fabric and remove the selvages first.

Layering and Basting

Unlike many machine quilters, I prefer to hand baste with thread rather than pin baste. This allows me to machine quilt without having to stop to remove pins.

1. Carefully press the quilt top from the back to set the seams and then press from the front. Press the backing. If you wish, use spray starch or sizing.

2. Spread the backing wrong side up on a clean, flat surface and secure it with masking tape. The fabric should be taut but not stretched. Center the batting over the backing and secure in place. Finally, center the quilt top over the batting.

3. Thread a long needle with light-colored thread. Beginning in the center of the quilt, stitch a 4″ grid of horizontal and vertical lines.

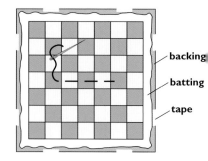

4. When you've finished basting, remove the tape and get ready to quilt!

QUILTING YOUR QUILT

A quilt becomes a quilt when it includes three layers—a top, a filler layer or batting, and a backing—all attached with stitching of some type to hold the layers together. (This means that to call your project a quilt, you need to finish it!) My quilts in this book—as well as almost all the quilts made by my wonderful group of quilters—are machine quilted.

Machine quilting is an art form, so there is a learning curve involved. Practice is the best way to learn and master this skill. Here are some guidelines to get you started.

Dual-Feed Foot

Use a dual-feed foot for straight-line quilting.

The dual-feed foot (page 6) is designed to hold and feed the three layers of your quilt even as you stitch. Use this foot to stitch single or parallel lines and grids—whether vertical, horizontal, or diagonal. You can also use this foot for certain decorative stitches and embellishing techniques, such as couching (page 67), to machine quilt.

Open-Toe Stippling Foot

Use an open-toe foot for free-motion quilting.

Also called a darning foot, the open-toe stippling foot (page 6) allows you to quilt in all directions: you are the guide! Use this foot for stipple quilting, meandering, and other free-motion techniques. I like to stipple quilt around machine-embroidered motifs, because this causes the embroidered design to pop out and become a focal point.

You will need to drop the feed dogs on your sewing machine when you use the open-toe stippling foot. You might also need to set the presser foot pressure to the darning position so you can move the quilt at a smooth pace for consistent stitches. Some machines have a built-in stipple stitch, which is a wonderful way to achieve this beautiful surface texture.

Threads

Typical thread choices for machine quilting include rayon (35- and 40-weight), cotton, polyester, and monofilament. I use lots of variegated and metallic threads, as well as novelty threads, such as Twister Tweeds, Swirling Sensation, and Moon Glow. The latter are manufactured by Robison-Anton (see Resources on page 72).

Design

There is a great deal going on in these Mariner's Medallion quilts, so you will probably want to keep the quilting fairly subtle in the heavily pieced areas. Save the showcase patterns for the open areas of your quilt, such as the compass background square and the various unpieced borders. Intricate rope and cable designs, for example, are especially appropriate border choices for these nautically themed quilts.

Begin by anchoring key seams in and around blocks and borders by stitching in-the-ditch along the seamlines. Try filling in open spaces with loops, curves, clamshells, and waves. Combine straight and curvy lines for variety.

I love to use heavy free-motion quilting, such as stippling, in the backgrounds behind pieced, appliquéd, and embroidered motifs. This causes the background to recede and the motif to pop forward, taking center stage in the design.

Note how the heavily quilted background in the Twinkle Star border of *My Canvas to the World* makes the stars seem to pop. (For a full view of this quilt, see page 59.)

If you have used the *same* fabric for both the compass background and the background square, try quilting both with a single filler quilting motif, such as stippling, to emphasize the illusion of the compass floating on the background. On the other hand, if you have chosen two *different* fabrics for the compass and square backgrounds, you might wish to leave the compass background unquilted—or quilt it simply with outline or in-the-ditch stitching—and choose a different, more elaborate pattern for the background square to emphasize the framing effect.

Don't overlook the design opportunities created by the compass points. Experiment with designs that radiate outward or that swirl in the background square, adding motion and excitement to the central compass motif.

One of my favorite options is to let the fabric inspire me. I can stitch a garden trellis over a floral fabric or add detail to a beach with quilted rocks and shells. I also love to pull a motif from the fabric and adapt it for quilting in another area of the quilt or, even more simply, to follow the fabric motif right where it is. The latter option is especially effective in a large-scale background or outer border fabric.

FINISHING YOUR QUILT

Your quilt's binding, hanging sleeve, and label are important too, so be sure to give them the same attention you've given to every other step of the process.

Squaring Up

Trim the excess batting and backing and square up your quilt. Use the seam of the outer border as a guide.

1. Align a ruler with the outer border seam and measure to the edge of the quilt in a number of places. Use the narrowest measurement as a guide for positioning your ruler and trim the excess batting and backing all around the quilt.

2. Fold the quilt in half lengthwise and crosswise to check that the corners are square and the sides are equal in length. If they aren't, use a large square ruler to correct this, one corner at a time.

Square up the corners.

3. Stabilize the quilt edges by stitching around the perimeter with a basting or serpentine stitch. (Do not use a zigzag stitch.)

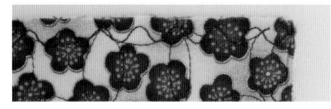

Serpentine stitch around quilt perimeter.

4. Remove any stray threads or bits of batting from the quilt top. You are now ready to bind your quilt.

Making and Applying Binding

The following method is the one I use to bind my quilts. It results in a finished edge that is attractive and strong.

1. Cut enough 3″-wide binding strips to go around the perimeter (outside edges) of the quilt, plus an extra 10″ for seams and corners. Sew the strips together at right angles, as shown. Trim the excess fabric, leaving a ¼″ seam allowance, and press the seams open.

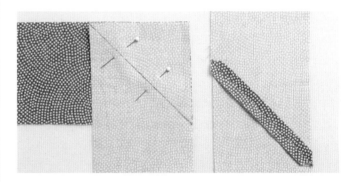

2. Fold the binding in half lengthwise, wrong sides together, and press.

3. Starting 6″ down from the upper right corner and with the raw edges even, place the binding on the quilt top. Check to see that none of the seams falls on a corner of the quilt. If one does, adjust the starting point. Begin stitching 4″ from the end of the binding, using a ½″ seam allowance.

4. Stitch about 2″, stop, and cut the threads. Remove the quilt from the machine and fold the binding to the back of the quilt. The binding should cover the line of machine stitching on the back. If the binding overlaps the stitching too much, try again, stitching just outside the first line of stitching. If the binding doesn't cover the original line of stitching, stitch just inside the line. Remove the unwanted stitches before you continue.

5. Using the position you determined for stitching in Step 4, resume stitching until you are ½″ from the first corner of the quilt. Stop, cut the thread, and remove the quilt from the machine.

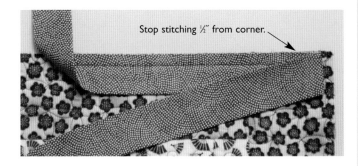

6. Fold the binding to create a mitered corner. Resume stitching, mitering each corner as you come to it.

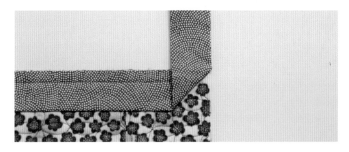

Stop stitching ½″ from corner.

7. Stop stitching about 3″ after you've turned the last corner. Make sure the starting and finishing ends of the binding overlap by at least 4″. Cut the threads and remove the quilt from the machine. Measure a 3″ overlap and trim the excess binding.

8. Place the quilt right side up. Unfold the unstitched tails, place them right sides together at right angles, and pin. Draw a line from the upper left corner to the lower right corner of the binding and stitch on the drawn line.

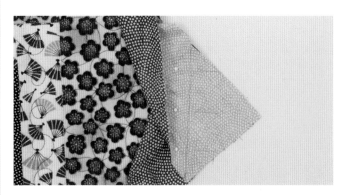

9. Carefully trim the seam allowance to ¼″ and press the seam open. Refold the binding and press. Finish stitching the binding to the quilt.

10. Turn the binding to the back of the quilt and pin. (I pin approximately 12″ at a time.) Use matching-colored thread to blindstitch the binding to the quilt back, carefully mitering the corners as you approach them. Hand stitch the miters on both sides.

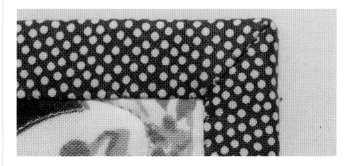

Making and Adding a Sleeve

If you want to display your quilt on a wall, you need to add a sleeve to protect your work of art from undue strain.

1. Cut an 8½″-wide strip of backing fabric 1″ shorter than the width of the quilt. (If the quilt is wider than 40″, cut 2 strips and stitch them together end to end.) Fold under the short ends ¼″; stitch and press.

2. Fold the sleeve lengthwise, right sides together. Sew the long raw edges and press. Turn the sleeve right side out and press again.

3. Match the center point of the top edge of the quilt with the center point of the sleeve. Pin the sleeve to the quilt, right below the binding. Use matching-colored thread to blindstitch the top edge in place.

4. Push up the bottom edge of the sleeve a tiny bit so that when inserted, the hanging rod does not put strain on the quilt. Blindstitch the bottom edge of the sleeve, taking care not to catch the front of the quilt as you stitch.

Creating a Label

I always recommend making a label for your quilt. This gives you a place to provide important information about both you and the quilt. You can sew the label to the lower right corner of the quilt back before it is quilted or wait to attach it after you complete the quilt.

I suggest including the following information on your label: the name of the quilt; your full name (and business name, if you have one); your city, county, province or state, and country of residence; and the date.

You can make a simple label by drawing and writing on fabric with permanent fabric markers. (Stabilize the fabric first with freezer paper or interfacing.) For a more elaborate (and fun!) label, try photo-transfer techniques, use the lettering system on your sewing machine, or use an embroidery machine to embellish your label. You can even create your own distinctive signature or logo.

Use the label to record key information about your quilt.

RESOURCES

SOURCES AND INFORMATION FOR PRODUCTS REFERENCED

For quilting supplies:
COTTON PATCH MAIL ORDER
3405 Hall Lane, Dept. CTB
Lafayette, CA 94549
(800) 835-4418
(925) 283-7883
quiltusa@yahoo.com
www.quiltusa.com

Note: Fabric manufacturers discontinue fabrics regularly. Exact fabrics shown may no longer be available.

For your nearest Husqvarna Viking dealer:
HUSQVARNA VIKING
www.husqvarnaviking.com

For information about thread:
ROBISON-ANTON TEXTILES
P.O. Box 159
Fairview, NJ 07022
(201) 941-0500
www.robison-anton.com

For information about Sulky KK 2000 and other Sulky products:
SULKY OF AMERICA
P.O. Box 494129
Port Charlotte, FL 33949-4129
(800) 874-4115
Fax: (941) 743-4634
info@sulky.com

For *Simple Foundation Translucent Vellum Paper* (for tracing and sewing foundation designs) and the *Quick & Easy Block Tool*:
Check your local quilt shop or favorite online source or refer to the C&T Publishing website: www.ctpub.com

EMBROIDERY COLLECTIONS

These and other embroidery collections are available at your local participating Husqvarna Viking or Pfaff sewing machine dealer.

My Favorite Quilt Designs, by M'Liss Rae Hawley, Disk Part #756 253300, *Inspira* collection, multiformat CD-ROM

Spring View, by M'Liss Rae Hawley, Disk Part #756 255100, *Inspira* collection, multiformat CD-ROM

Kimono Art, by M'Liss Rae Hawley, Disk Part #756 259800, *Inspira* collection, multiformat CD-ROM

Kimono Art II, by M'Liss Rae Hawley, Disk Part #620037296, *inspira* collection, multiformat CD-ROM

Up, Up, and Away, EZSewDesigns, Disk Part #756 105300, *Inspira* collection, multiformat CD-ROM

Flowers, Embroidery 12, Husqvarna Viking

Petite Paisley, by Margit Grimm, Embroidery 79, Husqvarna Viking

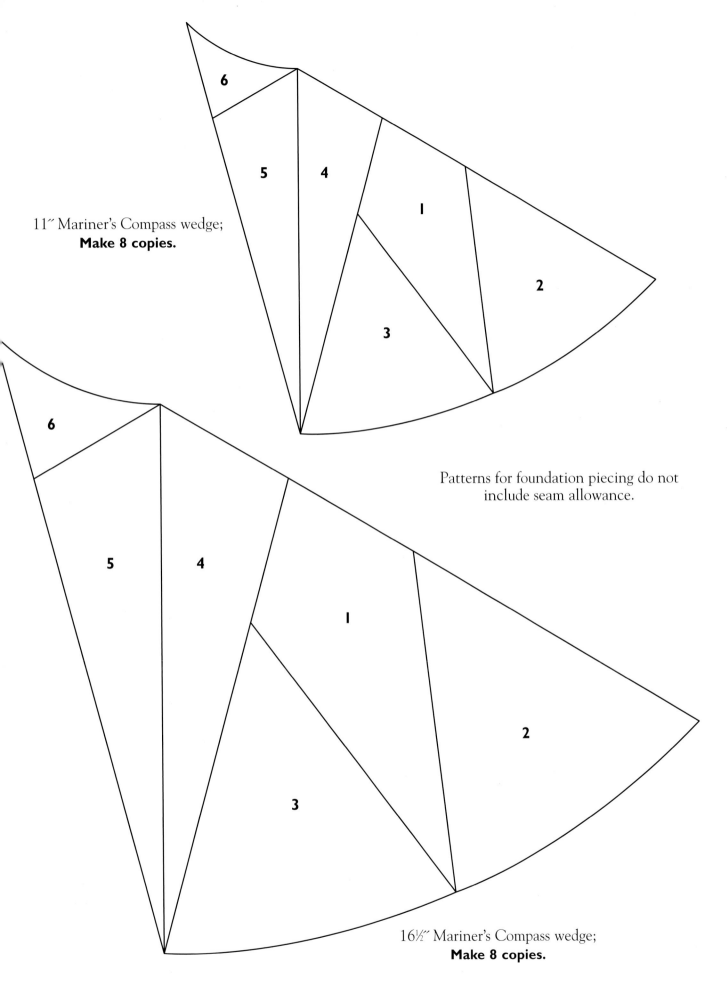

11″ Mariner's Compass wedge;
Make 8 copies.

Patterns for foundation piecing do not
include seam allowance.

16½″ Mariner's Compass wedge;
Make 8 copies.

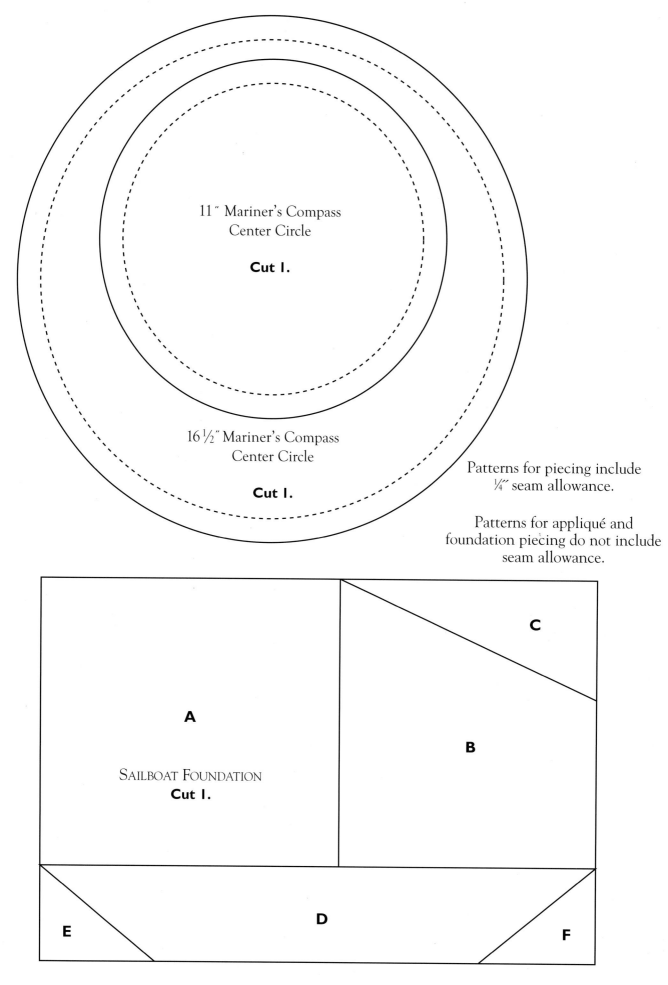

11″ Mariner's Compass
Center Circle

Cut 1.

16½″ Mariner's Compass
Center Circle

Cut 1.

Patterns for piecing include
¼″ seam allowance.

Patterns for appliqué and
foundation piecing do not include
seam allowance.

C

B

A

SAILBOAT FOUNDATION
Cut 1.

E

D

F

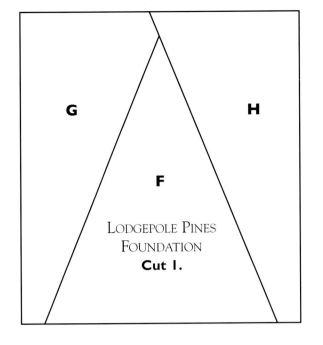

G **H**

F

LODGEPOLE PINES
FOUNDATION
Cut 1.

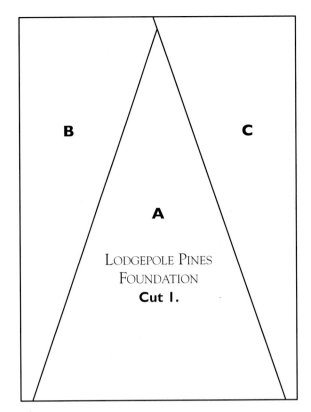

B **C**

A

LODGEPOLE PINES
FOUNDATION
Cut 1.

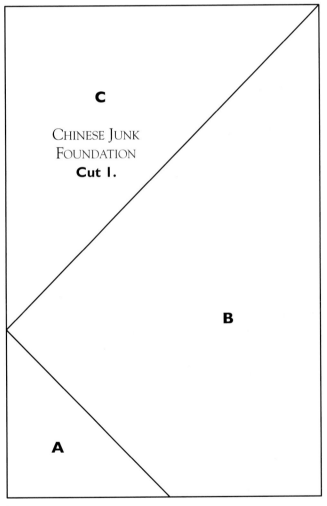

C

CHINESE JUNK
FOUNDATION
Cut 1.

B

A

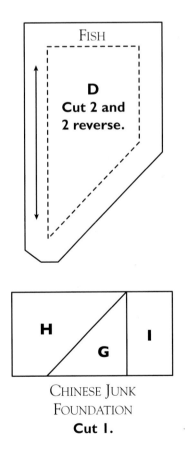

FISH

D
**Cut 2 and
2 reverse.**

H **I**

G

CHINESE JUNK
FOUNDATION
Cut 1.

CHINESE JUNK FOUNDATION
Cut 1.

E **D** **F**

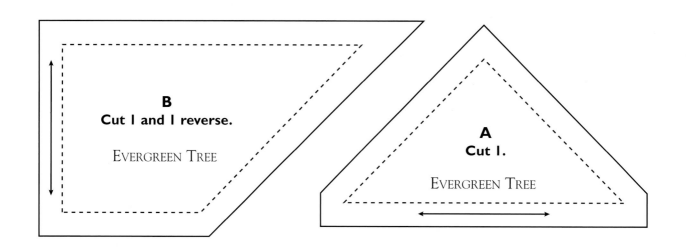

B
Cut 1 and 1 reverse.

EVERGREEN TREE

A
Cut 1.

EVERGREEN TREE

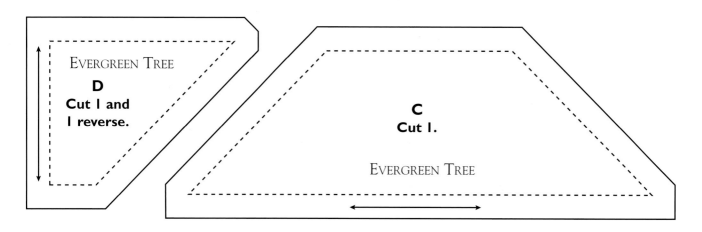

EVERGREEN TREE
D
Cut 1 and 1 reverse.

C
Cut 1.

EVERGREEN TREE

Patterns for piecing include
¼″ seam allowance.

Patterns for appliqué and foundation
piecing do not include seam allowance.

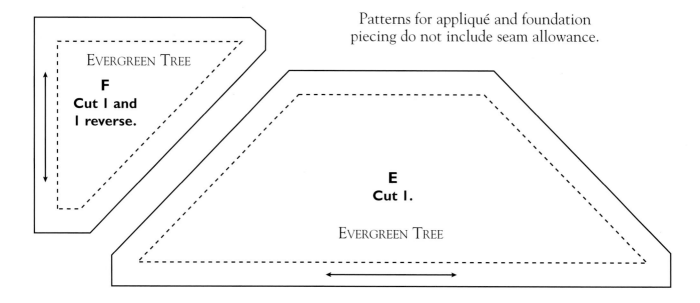

EVERGREEN TREE
F
Cut 1 and 1 reverse.

E
Cut 1.

EVERGREEN TREE

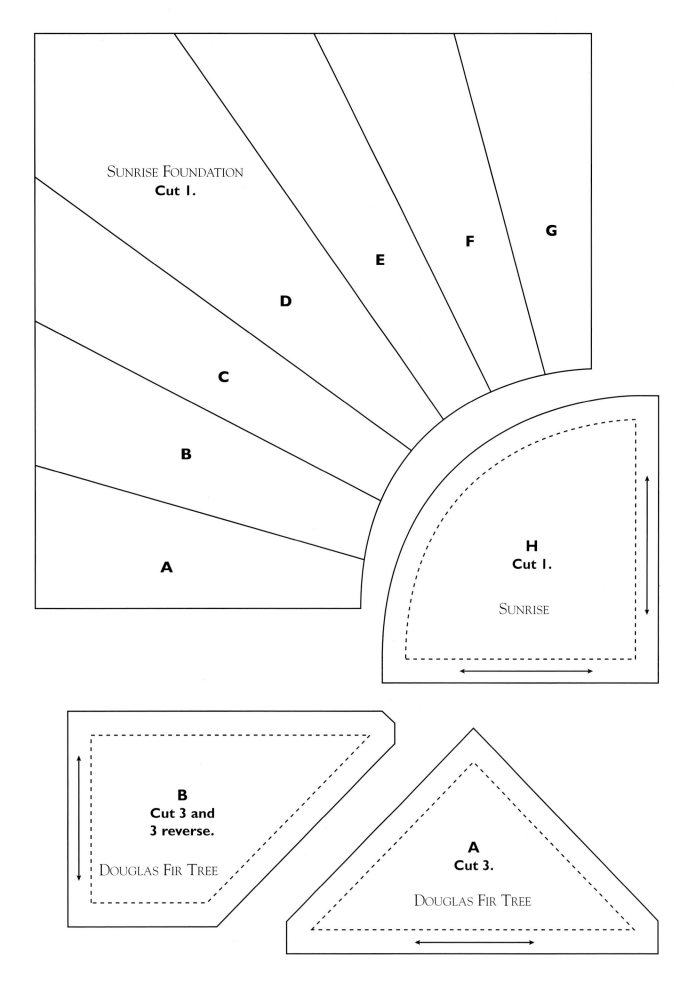

SUNRISE FOUNDATION
Cut 1.

G

F

E

D

C

B

A

H
Cut 1.

SUNRISE

B
**Cut 3 and
3 reverse.**

DOUGLAS FIR TREE

A
Cut 3.

DOUGLAS FIR TREE

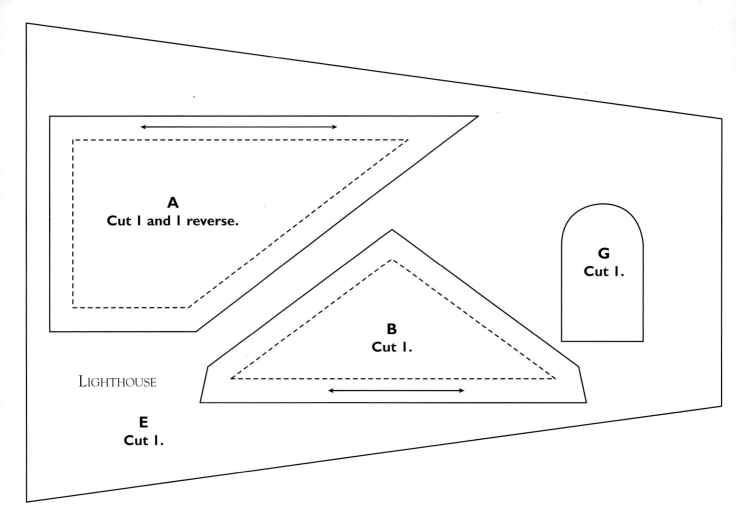

A
Cut 1 and 1 reverse.

G
Cut 1.

B
Cut 1.

LIGHTHOUSE

E
Cut 1.

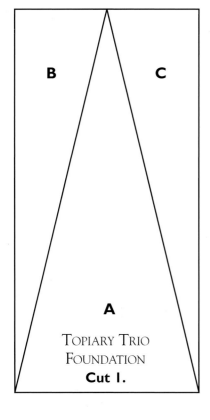

B   **C**

A

TOPIARY TRIO
FOUNDATION
Cut 1.

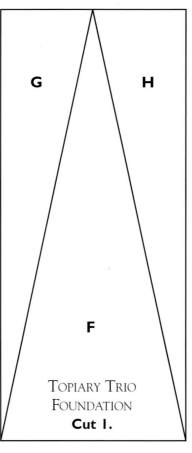

G   **H**

F

TOPIARY TRIO
FOUNDATION
Cut 1.

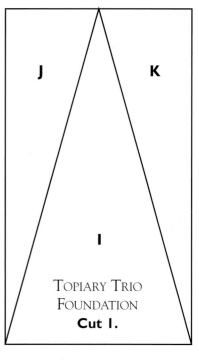

J   **K**

I

TOPIARY TRIO
FOUNDATION
Cut 1.